GRAPHIC BIOGRAPHIES

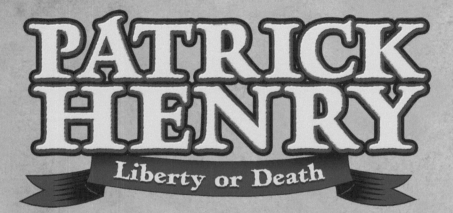

PATRICK HENRY

Liberty or Death

by Jason Glaser
illustrated by Peter McDonnell

Consultant:

Wayne Bodle, PhD

Assistant Professor of History

Indiana University of Pennsylvania

Capstone press

Mankato, Minnesota

Graphic Library is published by Capstone Press,
1710 Roe Crest Drive, North Mankato, Minnesota 56003.
www.capstonepub.com

Library of Congress Cataloging-in-Publication Data
Glaser, Jason.
Patrick Henry: liberty or death / by Jason Glaser; illustrated by Peter McDonnell.
p. cm.—(Graphic library. Graphic biographies)
Summary: "In graphic novel format, tells the life story of Patrick Henry, who is known as the 'Voice of the American Revolution.'"—Provided by publisher.
Includes bibliographical references and index.
ISBN: 978-0-7368-4970-8 (hardcover)
ISBN: 978-0-7368-6200-4 (paperback)
1. Henry, Patrick, 1736–1799—Juvenile literature. 2. Legislators—United States—Biography—Juvenile literature. 3. United States. Continental Congress—Biography—Juvenile literature. 4. Virginia—Politics and government—1775–1783—Juvenile literature. 5. United States—Politics and government—1775–1783—Juvenile literature. I. McDonnell, Peter, ill. II. Title. III. Series.
E302.6.H5G59 2006
973.3'092—dc22 2005004011

Art and Editorial Direction
Jason Knudson and Blake A. Hoena

Designers
Bob Lentz and Linda Clavel

Editor
Christopher Harbo

Editor's note: Direct quotations from primary sources are indicated by a yellow background.

Direct quotations appear on the following pages:
Pages 12, 14 (right), from *Patrick Henry: Patriot in the Making* by Robert Douthat Meade (Philadelphia: J. B. Lippincott Company, 1957).
Page 14 (left), from *Patrick Henry and His World* by George F. Willison (Garden City, N.Y.: Doubleday and Company, 1969).
Pages 15, 27, from *Patrick Henry: Practical Revolutionary* by Robert Douthat Meade (Philadelphia: J. B. Lippincott Company, 1969).
Page 25, from *Patrick Henry* by Moses Coit Tyler (Ithaca, N.Y.: Great Seal Books, 1962).

Printed in the United States 4941

TABLE OF CONTENTS

Chapter 1
Finding His Path

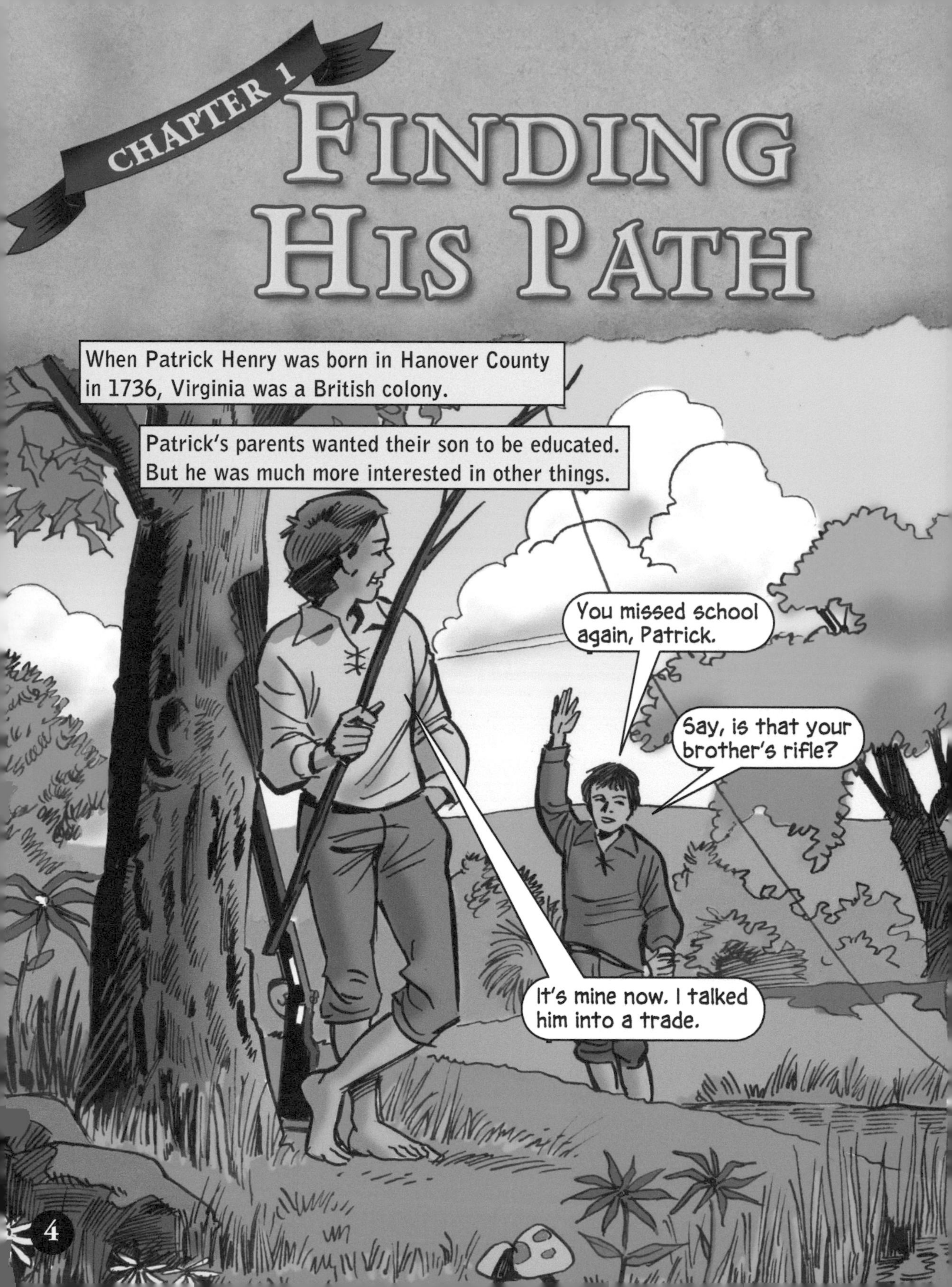
When Patrick Henry was born in Hanover County in 1736, Virginia was a British colony.
Patrick's parents wanted their son to be educated. But he was much more interested in other things.
You missed school again, Patrick.
Say, is that your brother's rifle?
It's mine now. I talked him into a trade.

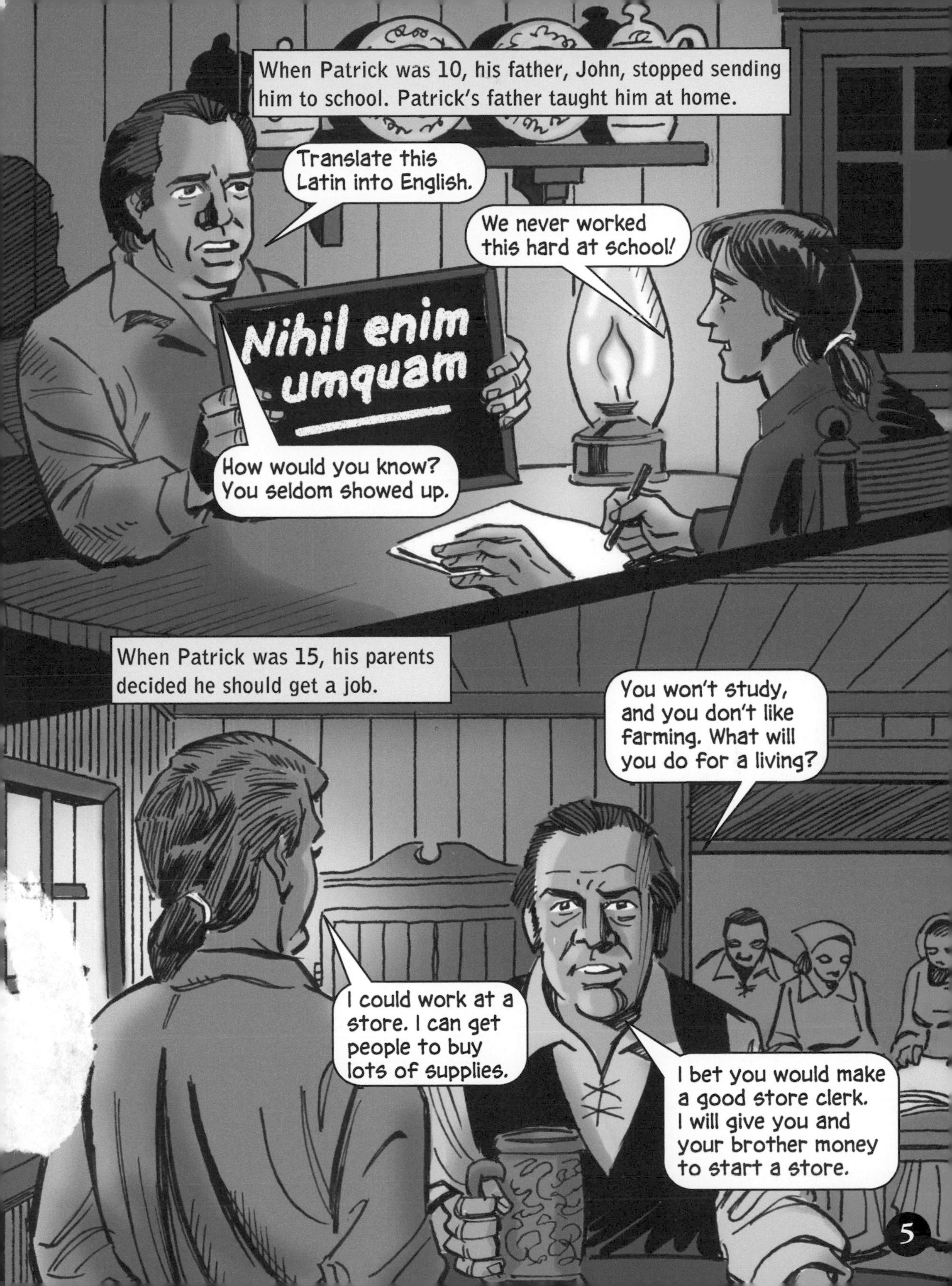
When Patrick was 10, his father, John, stopped sending him to school. Patrick's father taught him at home.
Translate this Latin into English.
Nihil enim umquam
We never worked this hard at school!
How would you know? You seldom showed up.
When Patrick was 15, his parents decided he should get a job.
You won't study, and you don't like farming. What will you do for a living?
I could work at a store. I can get people to buy lots of supplies.
I bet you would make a good store clerk. I will give you and your brother money to start a store.

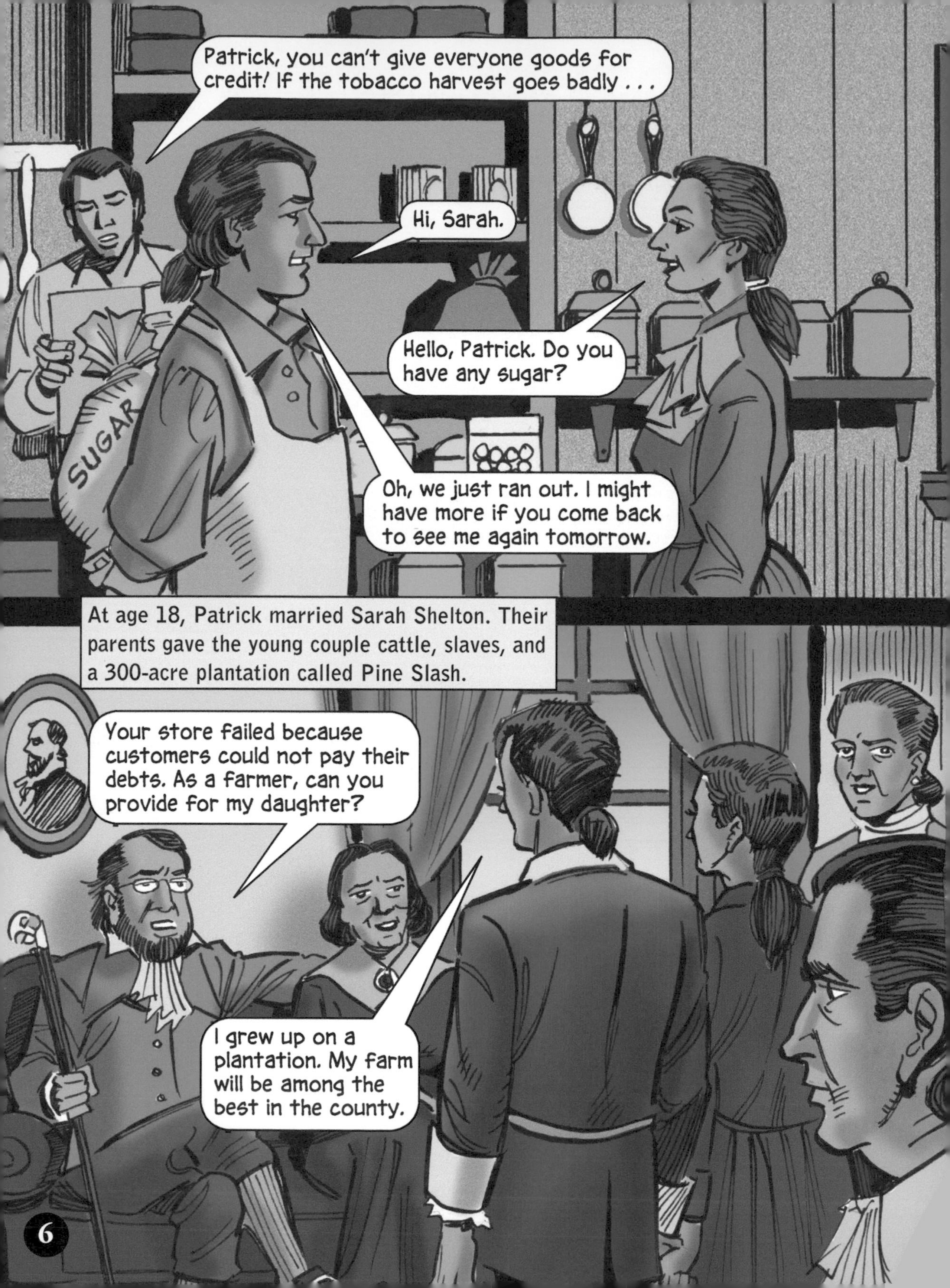
Patrick, you can't give everyone goods for credit! If the tobacco harvest goes badly . . .
Hi, Sarah.
Hello, Patrick. Do you have any sugar?
SUGAR
Oh, we just ran out. I might have more if you come back to see me again tomorrow.
At age 18, Patrick married Sarah Shelton. Their parents gave the young couple cattle, slaves, and a 300-acre plantation called Pine Slash.
Your store failed because customers could not pay their debts. As a farmer, can you provide for my daughter?
I grew up on a plantation. My farm will be among the best in the county.

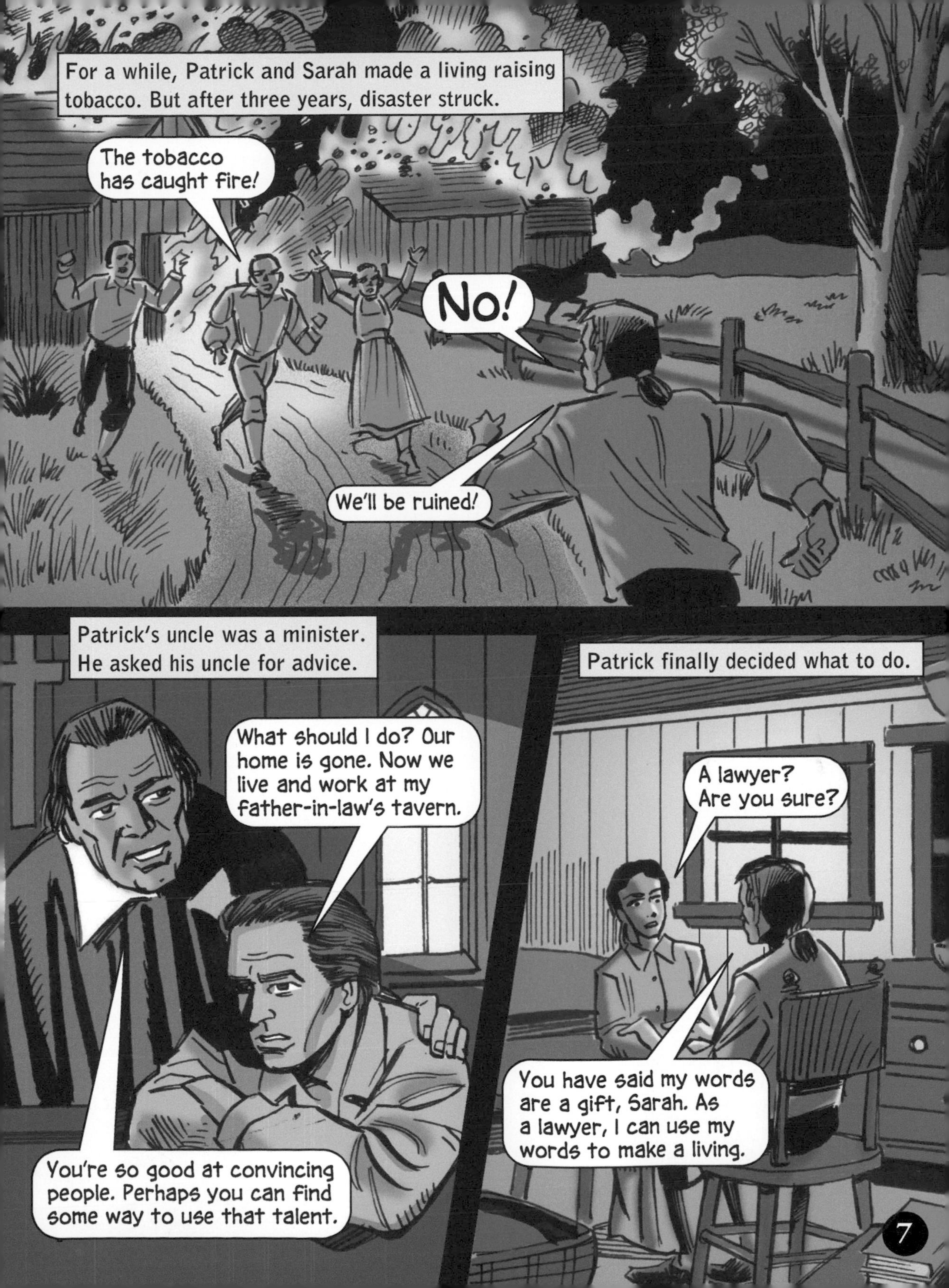
For a while, Patrick and Sarah made a living raising tobacco. But after three years, disaster struck.
The tobacco has caught fire!
No!
We'll be ruined!
Patrick's uncle was a minister. He asked his uncle for advice.
What should I do? Our home is gone. Now we live and work at my father-in-law's tavern.
You're so good at convincing people. Perhaps you can find some way to use that talent.
Patrick finally decided what to do.
A lawyer? Are you sure?
You have said my words are a gift, Sarah. As a lawyer, I can use my words to make a living.

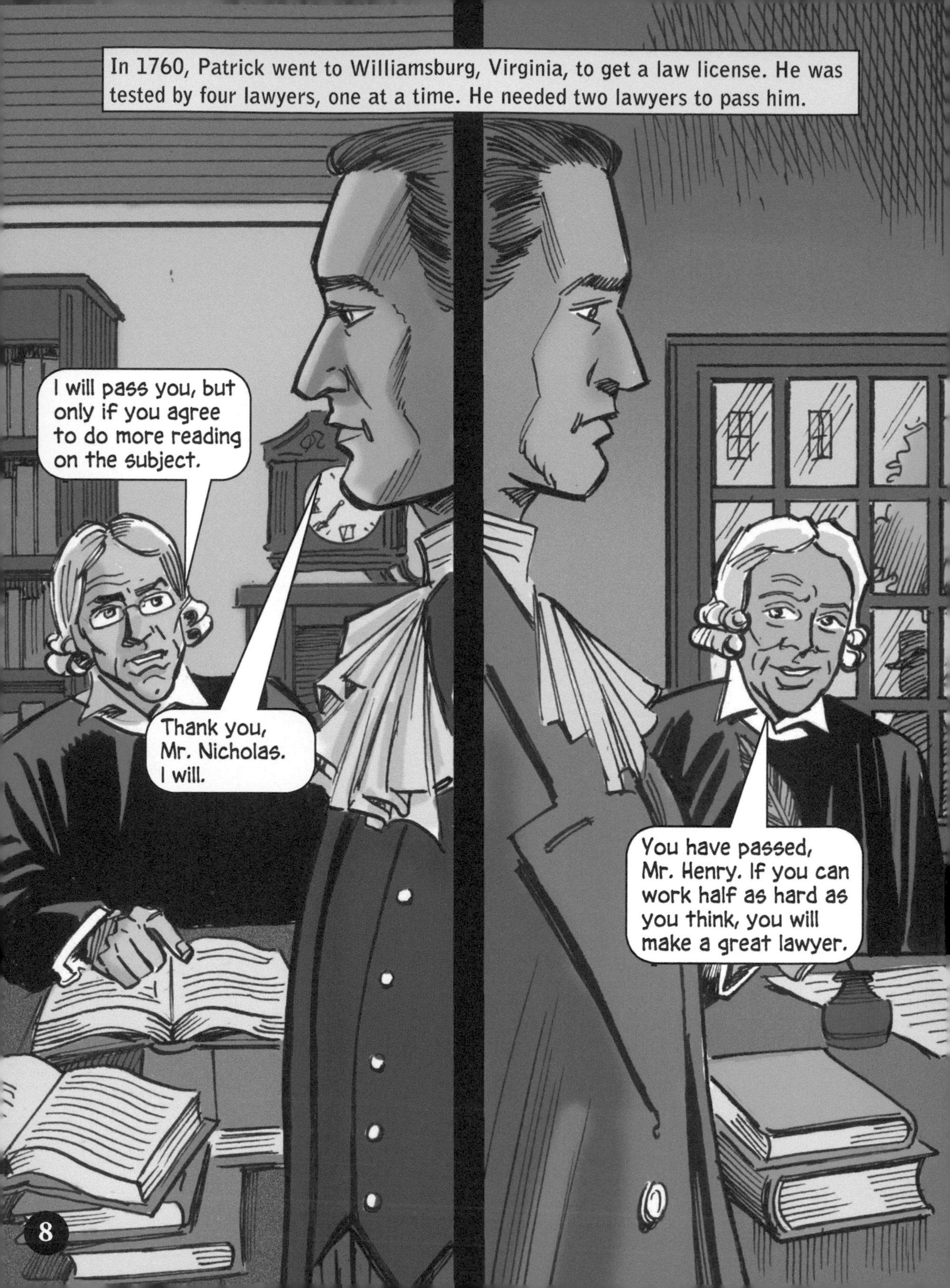
In 1760, Patrick went to Williamsburg, Virginia, to get a law license. He was tested by four lawyers, one at a time. He needed two lawyers to pass him.
I will pass you, but only if you agree to do more reading on the subject.
Thank you, Mr. Nicholas. I will.
You have passed, Mr. Henry. If you can work half as hard as you think, you will make a great lawyer.

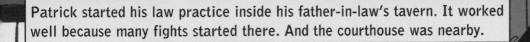

Patrick started his law practice inside his father-in-law's tavern. It worked well because many fights started there. And the courthouse was nearby.

You heard him. He called me a "hog stealer." I'll sue him!

Your case regarding public insult is strong, Mr. Henry. I award your client 20 pounds.

Patrick's arguments impressed many people. He soon became a popular lawyer.

My neighbor won't pay me what he owes me.

Henry! I need your help getting back some land.

I was sold a lame horse. Will you represent me?

9

CHAPTER 2

VOICE OF LIBERTY

In Virginia, British law said church ministers would be paid in tobacco. But in 1758, the tobacco harvest was poor. Virginia lawmakers passed a law saying ministers would be paid two pennies for each pound of tobacco they usually received. Ministers were outraged.

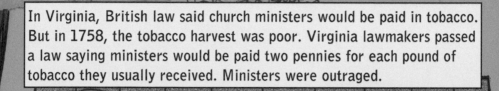

I could sell the tobacco owed me for more than two pennies a pound.

But Uncle, people must have freedom to change laws when times are tough.

You may think so, but Great Britain has rejected Virginia's two-penny law.

In the early 1760s, some ministers sued to get more money for their 1758 wages.

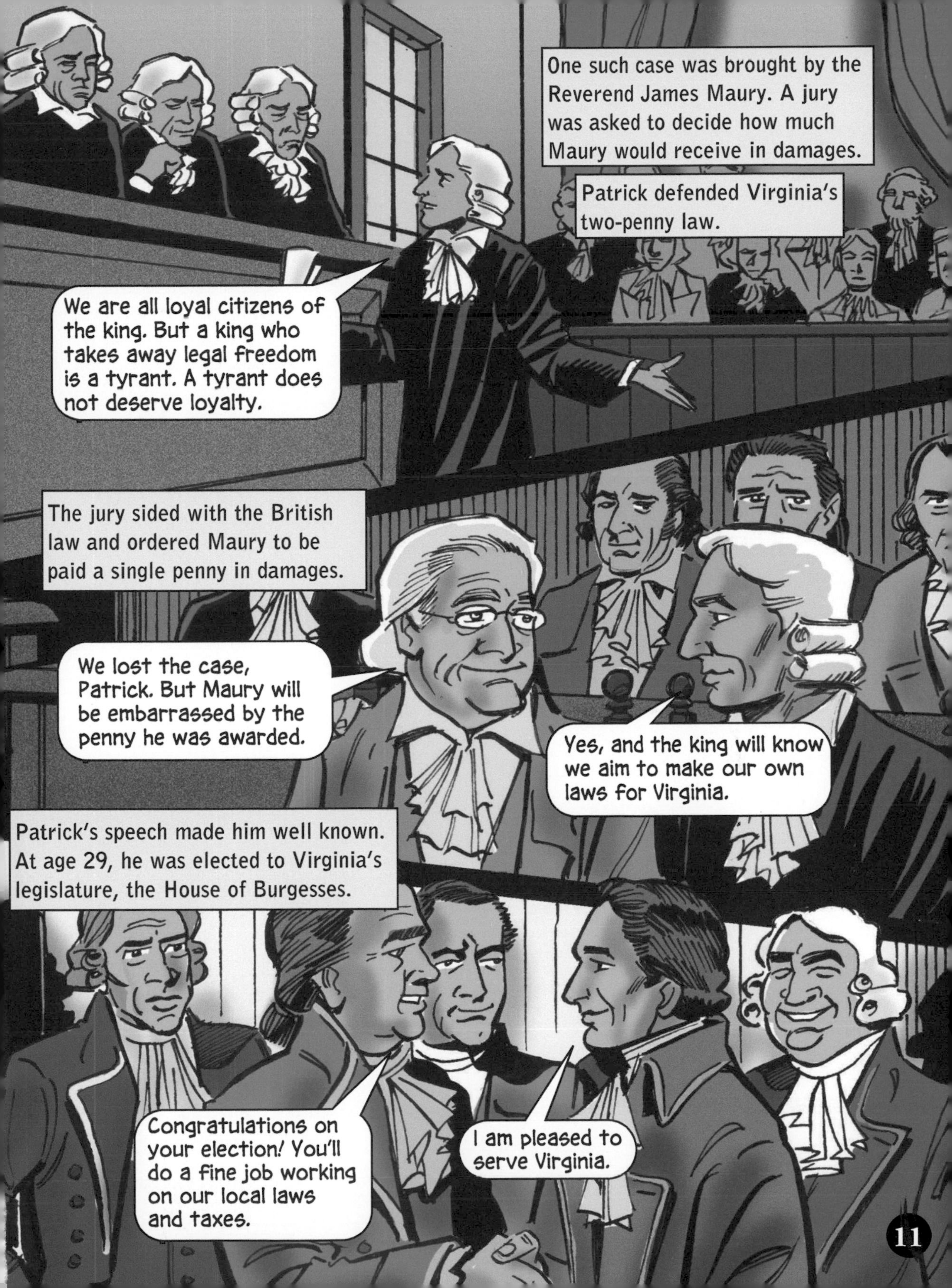

One such case was brought by the Reverend James Maury. A jury was asked to decide how much Maury would receive in damages.
Patrick defended Virginia's two-penny law.
We are all loyal citizens of the king. But a king who takes away legal freedom is a tyrant. A tyrant does not deserve loyalty.
The jury sided with the British law and ordered Maury to be paid a single penny in damages.
We lost the case, Patrick. But Maury will be embarrassed by the penny he was awarded.
Yes, and the king will know we aim to make our own laws for Virginia.
Patrick's speech made him well known. At age 29, he was elected to Virginia's legislature, the House of Burgesses.
Congratulations on your election! You'll do a fine job working on our local laws and taxes.
I am pleased to serve Virginia.

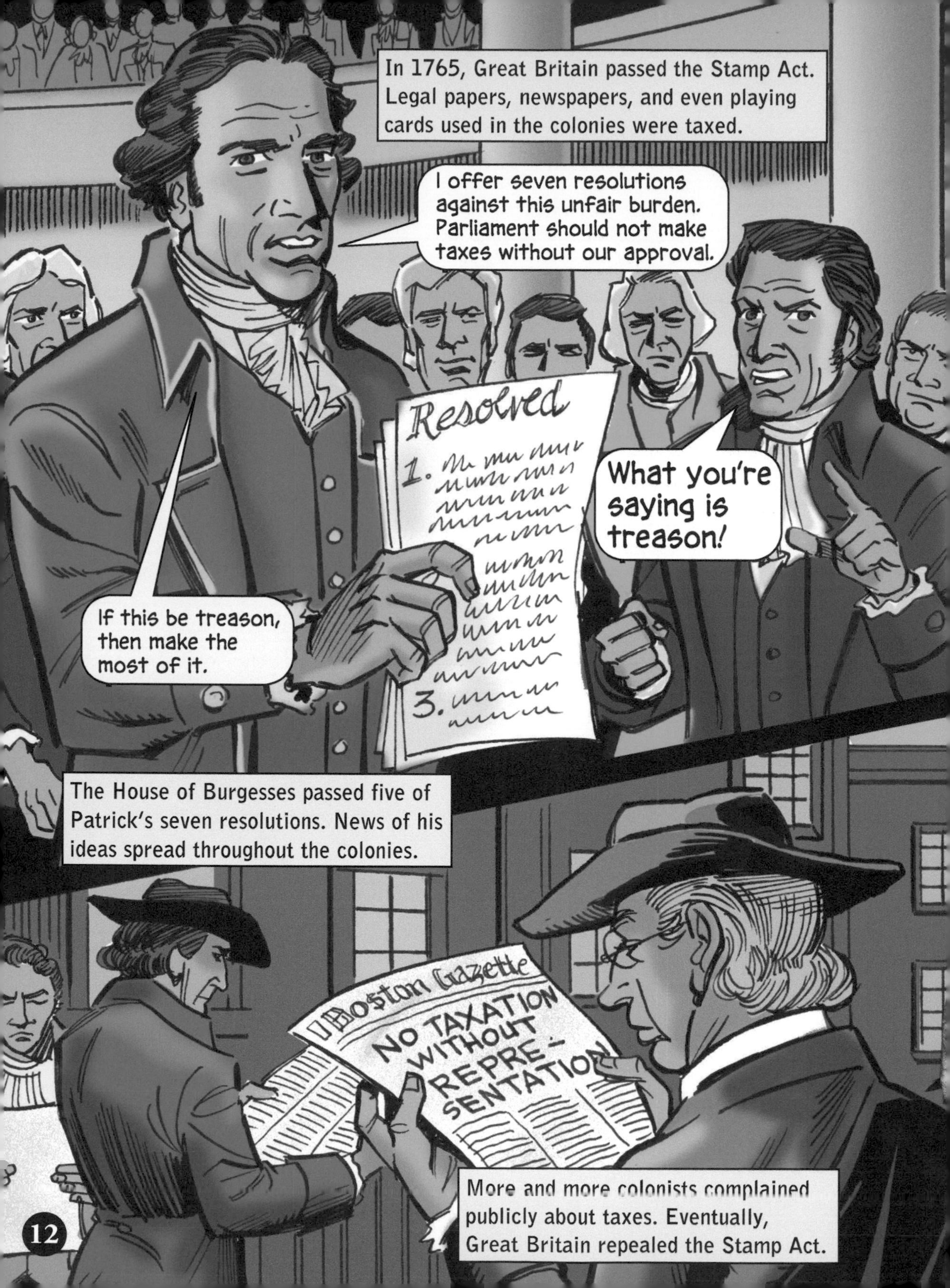
In 1765, Great Britain passed the Stamp Act. Legal papers, newspapers, and even playing cards used in the colonies were taxed.
I offer seven resolutions against this unfair burden. Parliament should not make taxes without our approval.
Resolved
1.
3.
What you're saying is treason!
If this be treason, then make the most of it.
The House of Burgesses passed five of Patrick's seven resolutions. News of his ideas spread throughout the colonies.
Boston Gazette
NO TAXATION WITHOUT REPRE-SENTATION
More and more colonists complained publicly about taxes. Eventually, Great Britain repealed the Stamp Act.

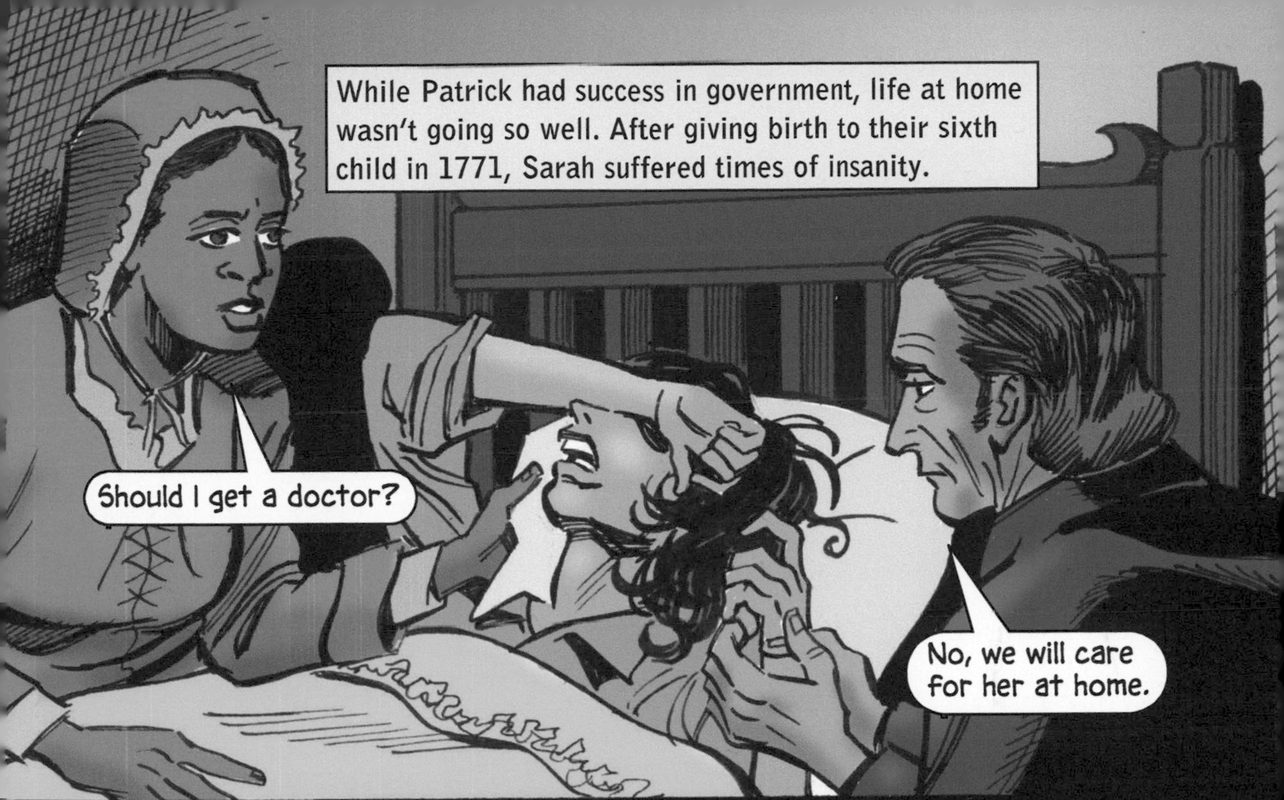
While Patrick had success in government, life at home wasn't going so well. After giving birth to their sixth child in 1771, Sarah suffered times of insanity.
Should I get a doctor?
No, we will care for her at home.

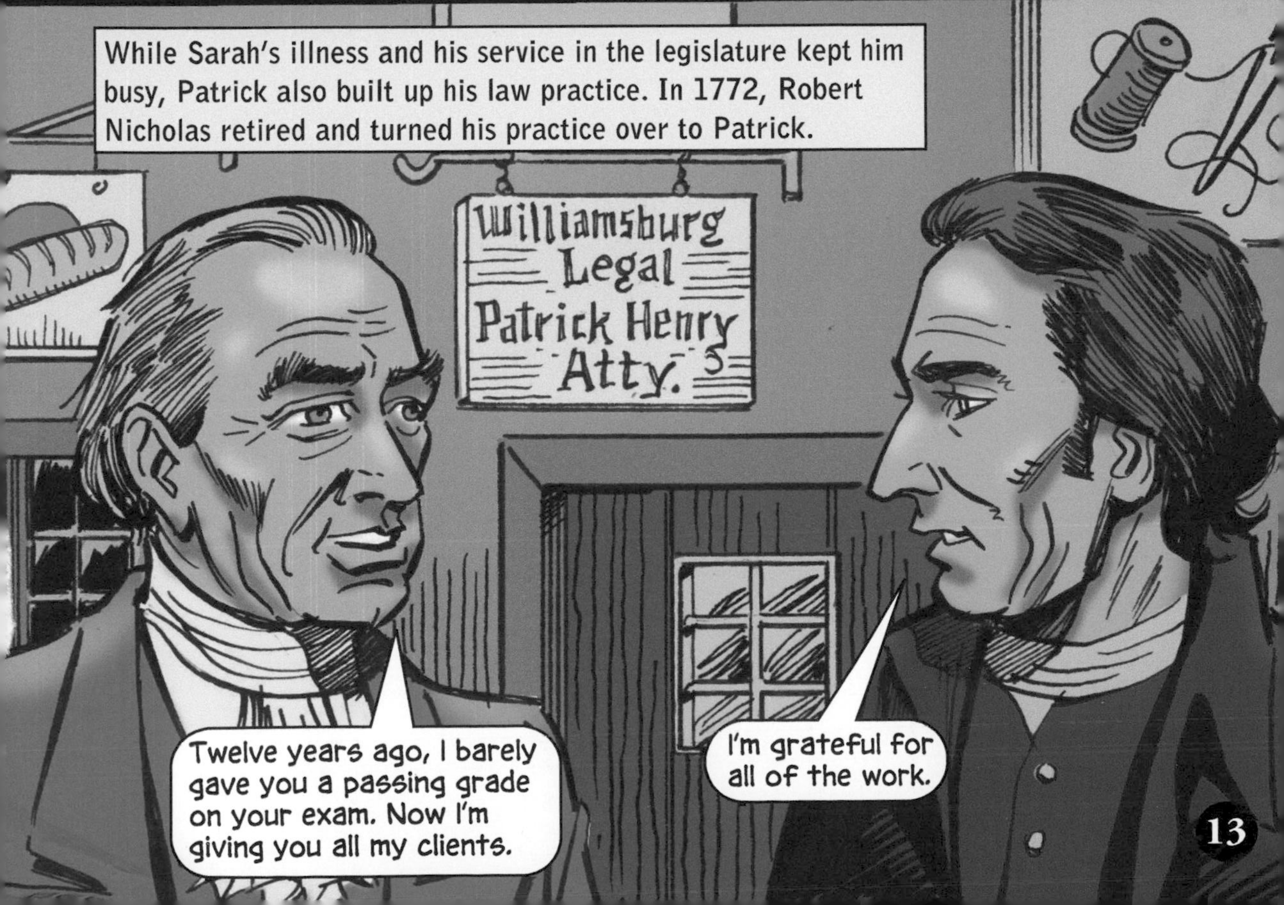
While Sarah's illness and his service in the legislature kept him busy, Patrick also built up his law practice. In 1772, Robert Nicholas retired and turned his practice over to Patrick.
Williamsburg Legal Patrick Henry Atty.
Twelve years ago, I barely gave you a passing grade on your exam. Now I'm giving you all my clients.
I'm grateful for all of the work.

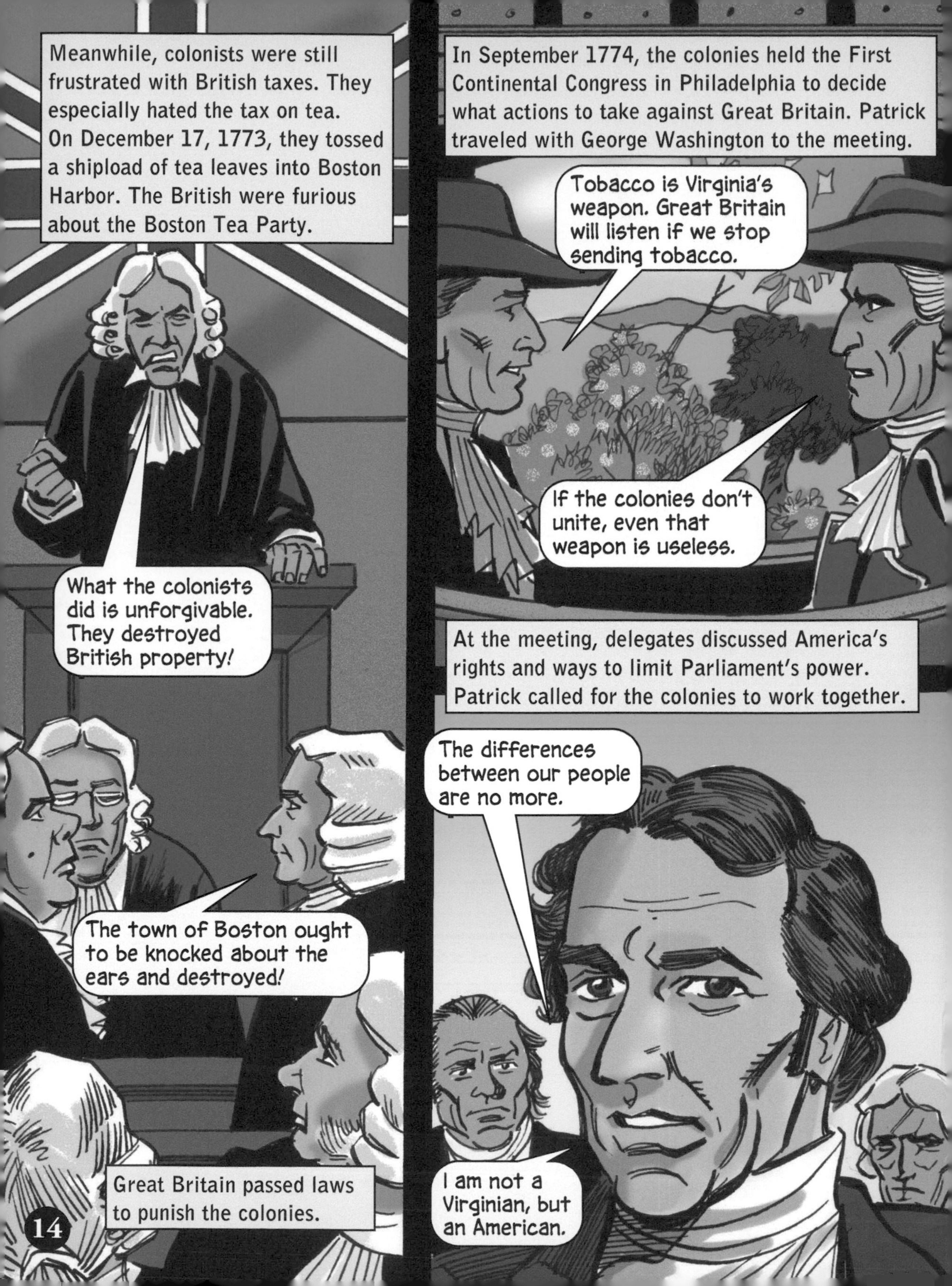
Meanwhile, colonists were still frustrated with British taxes. They especially hated the tax on tea. On December 17, 1773, they tossed a shipload of tea leaves into Boston Harbor. The British were furious about the Boston Tea Party.
What the colonists did is unforgivable. They destroyed British property!
The town of Boston ought to be knocked about the ears and destroyed!
Great Britain passed laws to punish the colonies.
In September 1774, the colonies held the First Continental Congress in Philadelphia to decide what actions to take against Great Britain. Patrick traveled with George Washington to the meeting.
Tobacco is Virginia's weapon. Great Britain will listen if we stop sending tobacco.
If the colonies don't unite, even that weapon is useless.
At the meeting, delegates discussed America's rights and ways to limit Parliament's power. Patrick called for the colonies to work together.
The differences between our people are no more.
I am not a Virginian, but an American.

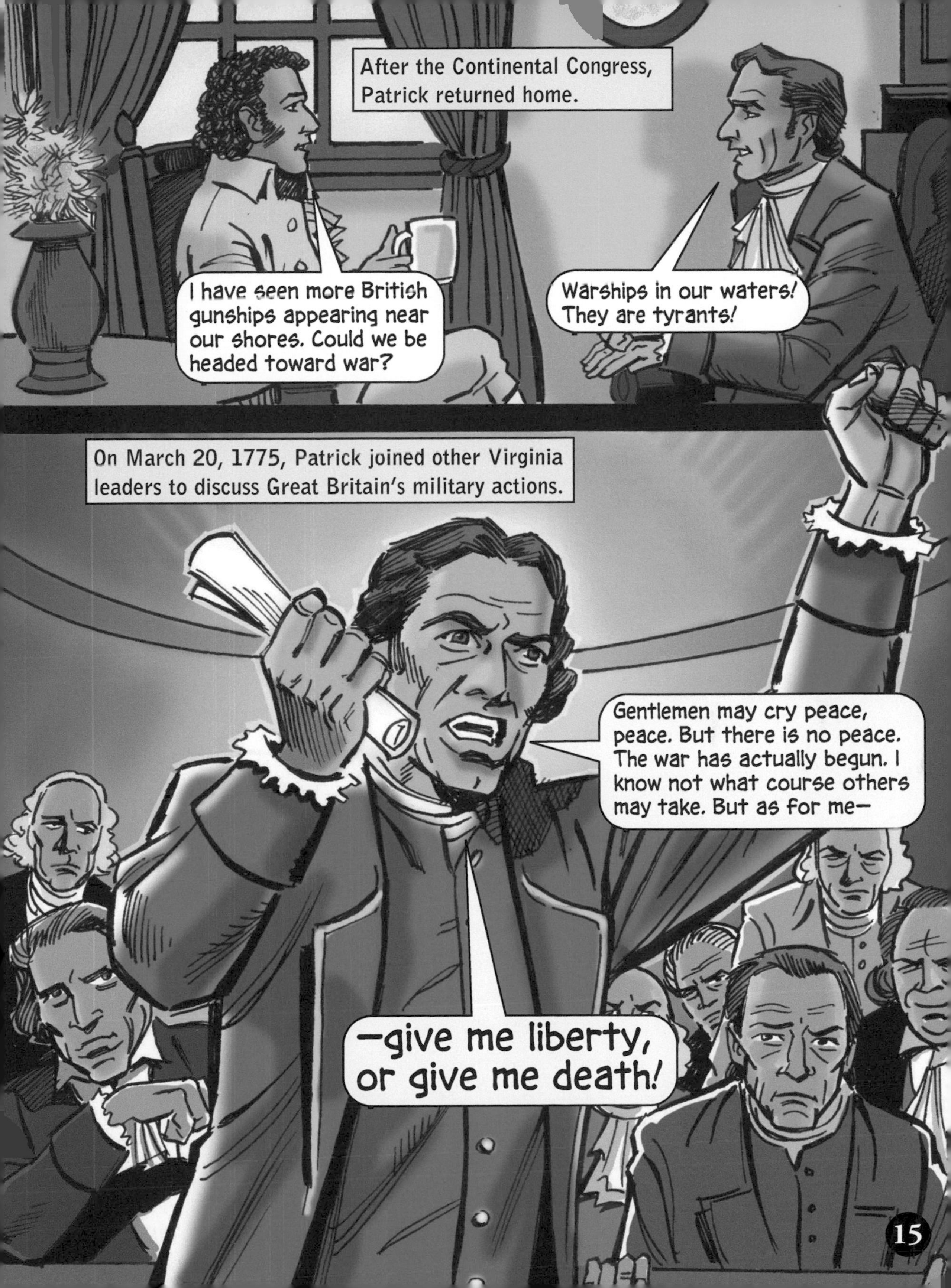
After the Continental Congress, Patrick returned home.
I have seen more British gunships appearing near our shores. Could we be headed toward war?
Warships in our waters! They are tyrants!
On March 20, 1775, Patrick joined other Virginia leaders to discuss Great Britain's military actions.
Gentlemen may cry peace, peace. But there is no peace. The war has actually begun. I know not what course others may take. But as for me—
—give me liberty, or give me death!

CHAPTER 3 WARTIME LEADER

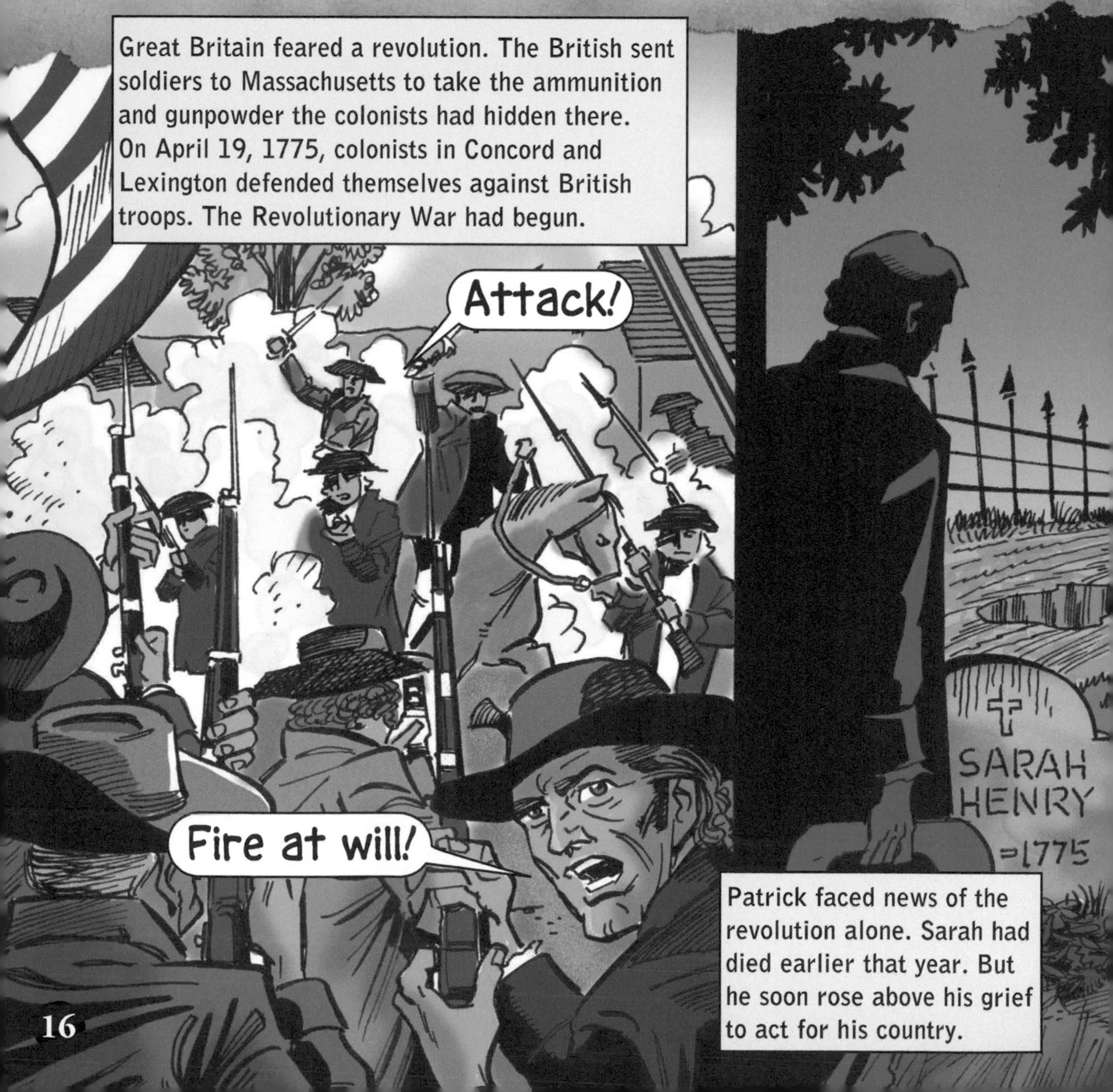
Great Britain feared a revolution. The British sent soldiers to Massachusetts to take the ammunition and gunpowder the colonists had hidden there. On April 19, 1775, colonists in Concord and Lexington defended themselves against British troops. The Revolutionary War had begun.
Attack!
Fire at will!
SARAH HENRY
-1775
Patrick faced news of the revolution alone. Sarah had died earlier that year. But he soon rose above his grief to act for his country.

In Virginia, Governor John Dunmore, who was loyal to Great Britain, took gunpowder stored in Virginia's capital city of Williamsburg.

We want the gunpowder the governor stole from the colony.

Patrick, the governor has agreed to pay you double what the gunpowder was worth. Just stop your march on Williamsburg.

Agreed.

Even though he agreed to pay for the gunpowder, Dunmore was furious.

Write this down . . .

Patrick Henry has taken a position of war. Do not aid him. Such actions risk punishment from the king.

Notice
Patrick
taken a
of war.

But Great Britain's control over the 13 colonies was slipping. In June, the governor fled to a British warship anchored off the coast.

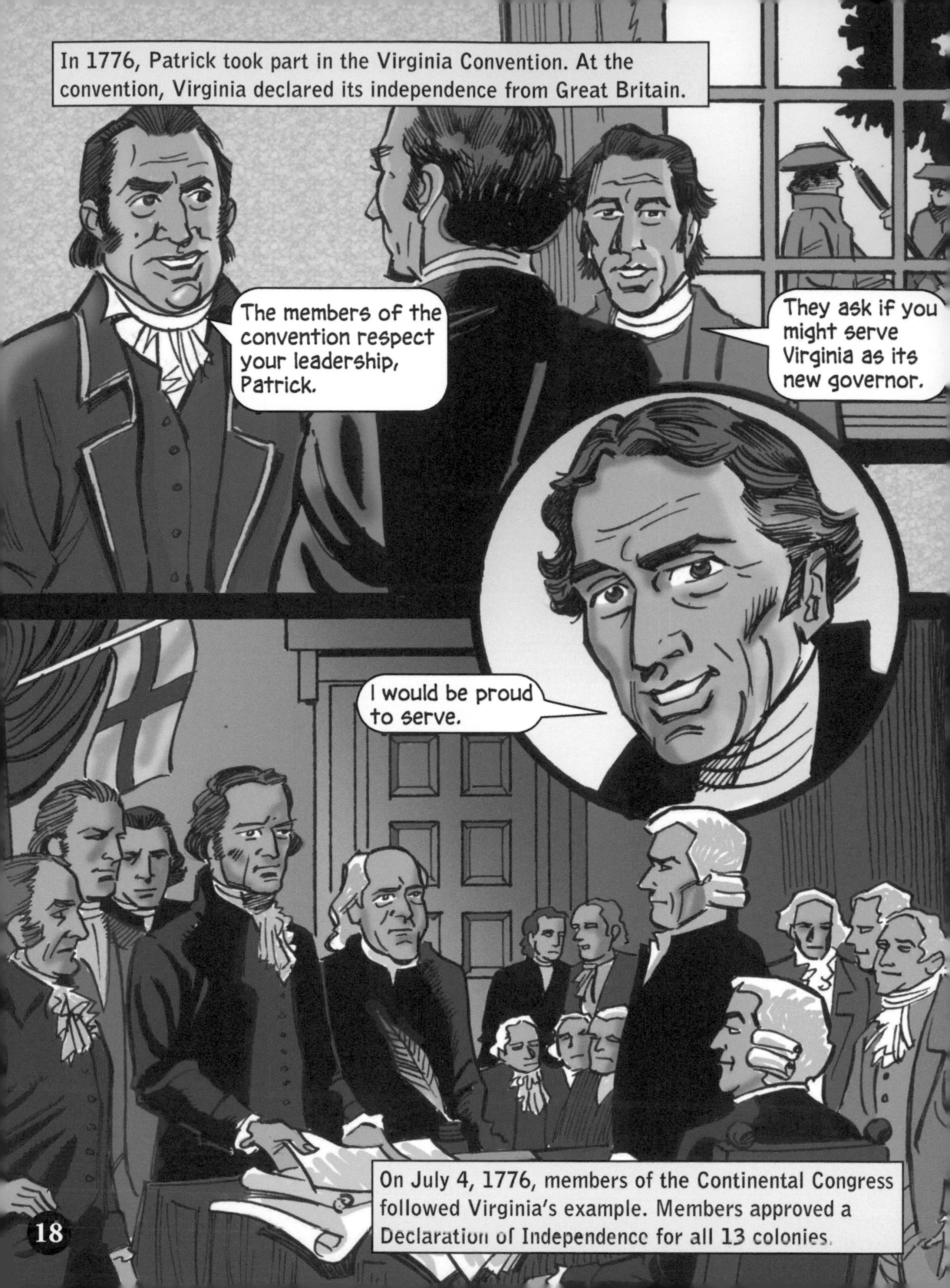
In 1776, Patrick took part in the Virginia Convention. At the convention, Virginia declared its independence from Great Britain.
The members of the convention respect your leadership, Patrick.
They ask if you might serve Virginia as its new governor.
I would be proud to serve.
On July 4, 1776, members of the Continental Congress followed Virginia's example. Members approved a Declaration of Independence for all 13 colonies.

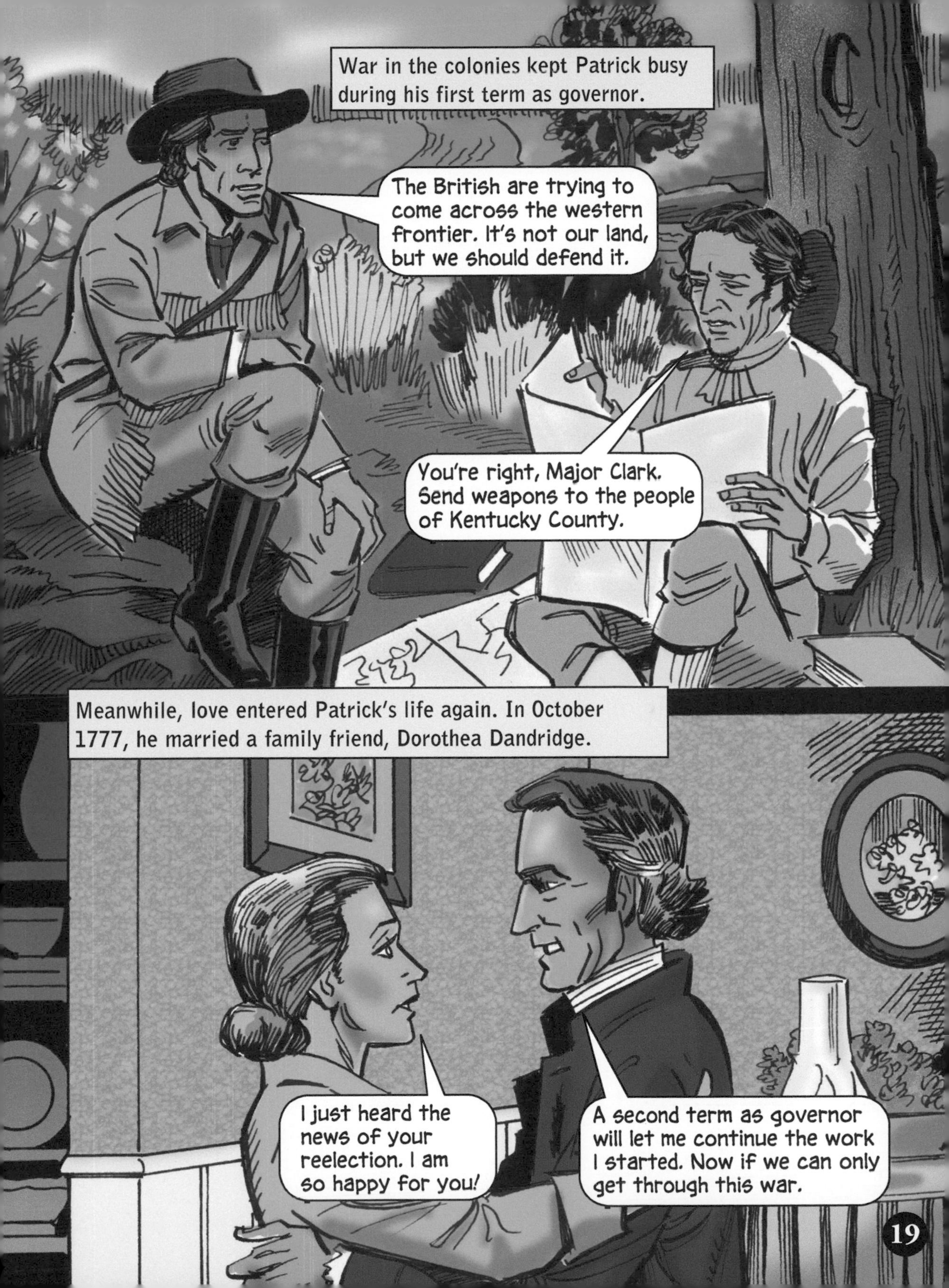
War in the colonies kept Patrick busy during his first term as governor.
The British are trying to come across the western frontier. It's not our land, but we should defend it.
You're right, Major Clark. Send weapons to the people of Kentucky County.
Meanwhile, love entered Patrick's life again. In October 1777, he married a family friend, Dorothea Dandridge.
I just heard the news of your reelection. I am so happy for you!
A second term as governor will let me continue the work I started. Now if we can only get through this war.

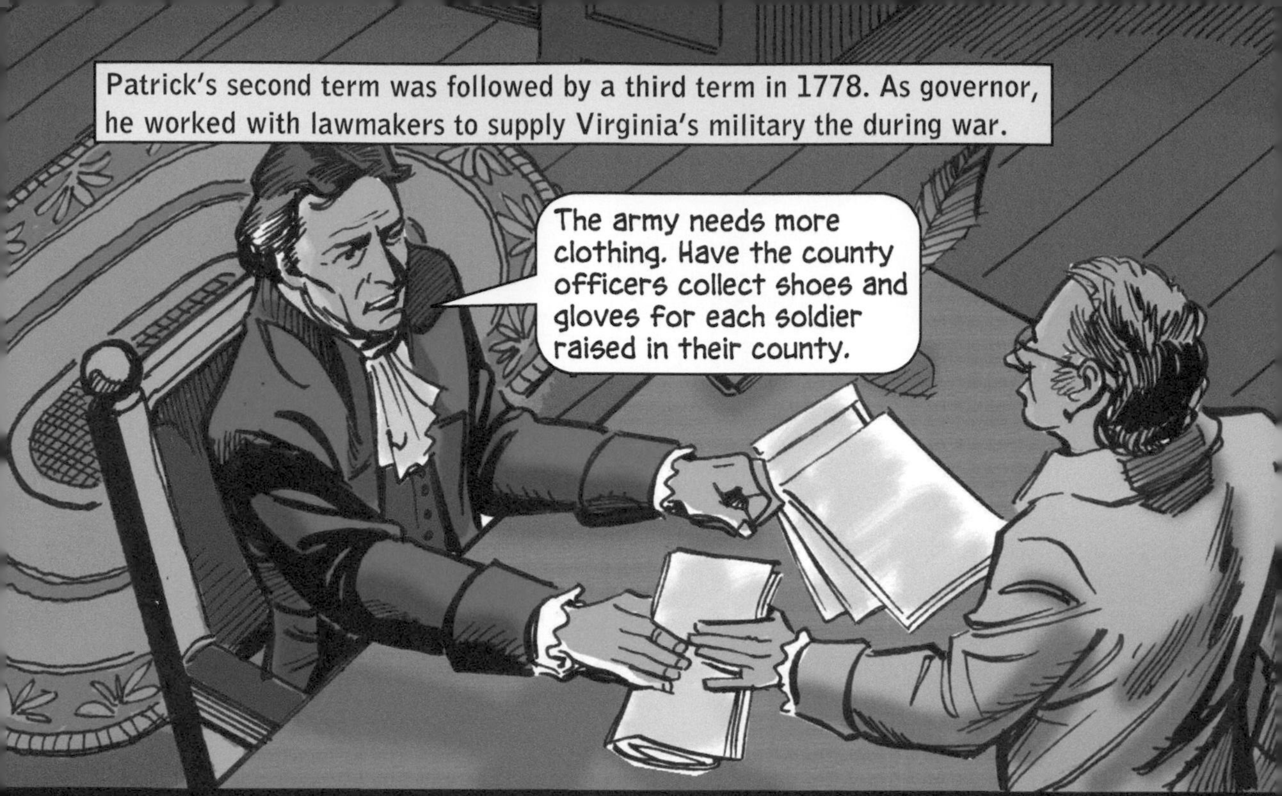
Patrick's second term was followed by a third term in 1778. As governor, he worked with lawmakers to supply Virginia's military the during war.
The army needs more clothing. Have the county officers collect shoes and gloves for each soldier raised in their county.

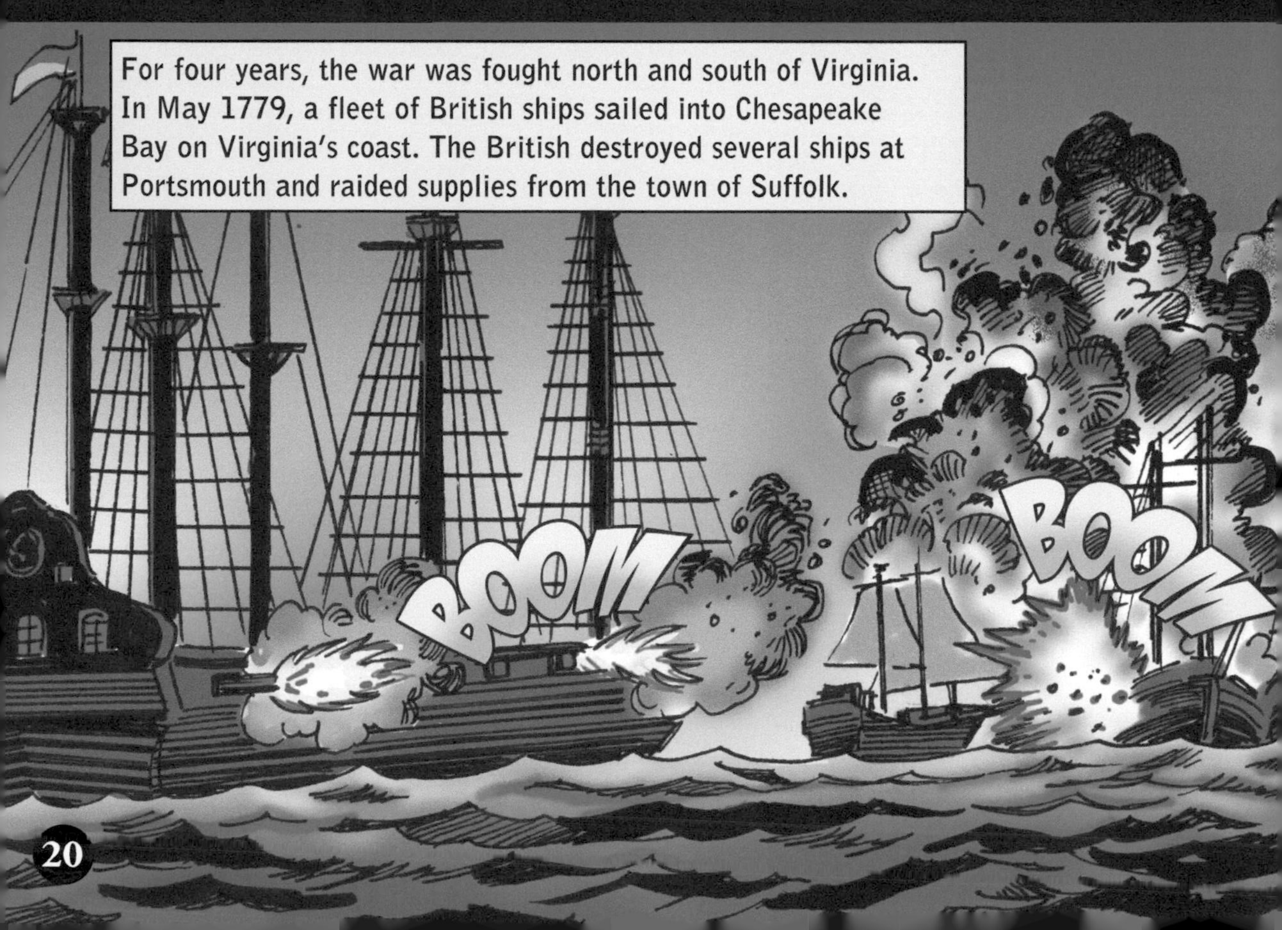
For four years, the war was fought north and south of Virginia. In May 1779, a fleet of British ships sailed into Chesapeake Bay on Virginia's coast. The British destroyed several ships at Portsmouth and raided supplies from the town of Suffolk.
BOOM
BOOM

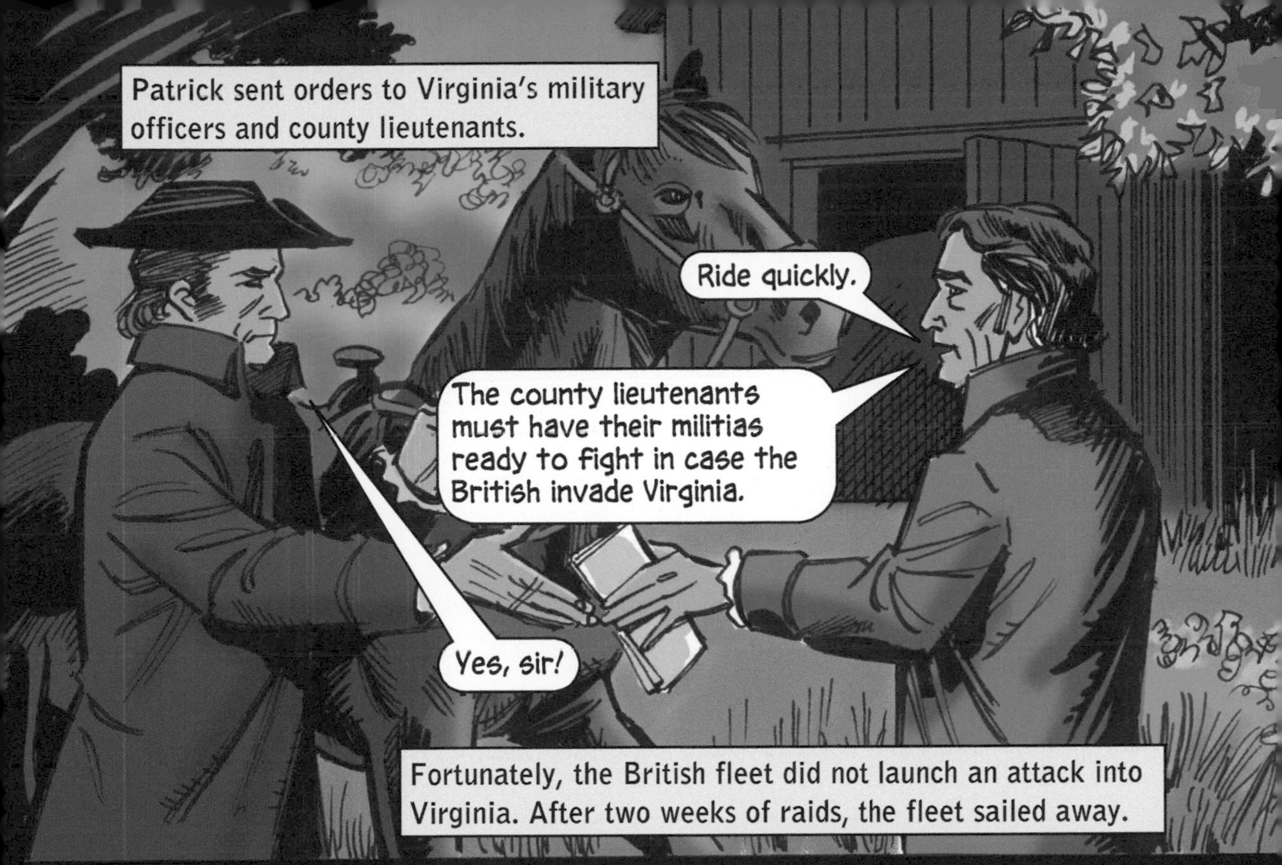
Patrick sent orders to Virginia's military officers and county lieutenants.
Ride quickly.
The county lieutenants must have their militias ready to fight in case the British invade Virginia.
Yes, sir!
Fortunately, the British fleet did not launch an attack into Virginia. After two weeks of raids, the fleet sailed away.

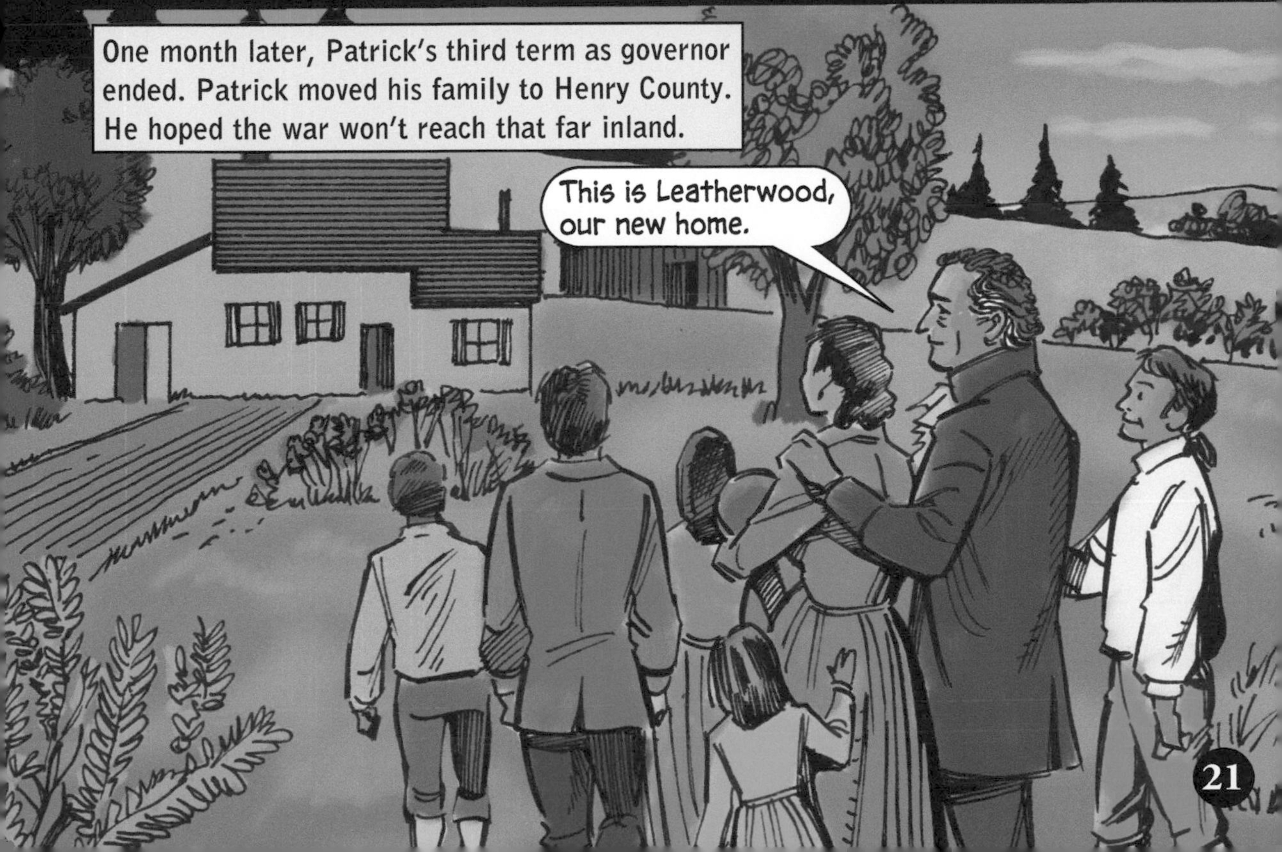
One month later, Patrick's third term as governor ended. Patrick moved his family to Henry County. He hoped the war won't reach that far inland.
This is Leatherwood, our new home.

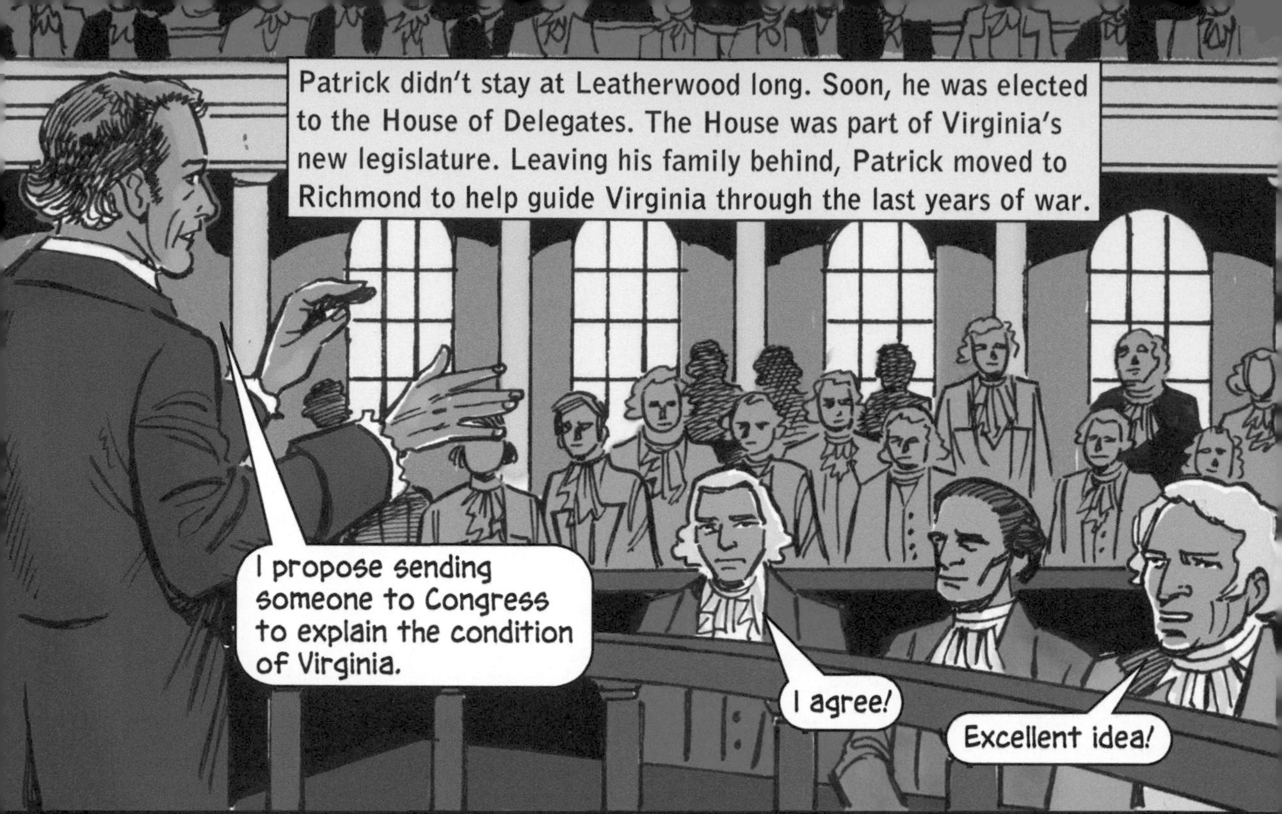
Patrick didn't stay at Leatherwood long. Soon, he was elected to the House of Delegates. The House was part of Virginia's new legislature. Leaving his family behind, Patrick moved to Richmond to help guide Virginia through the last years of war.
I propose sending someone to Congress to explain the condition of Virginia.
I agree!
Excellent idea!

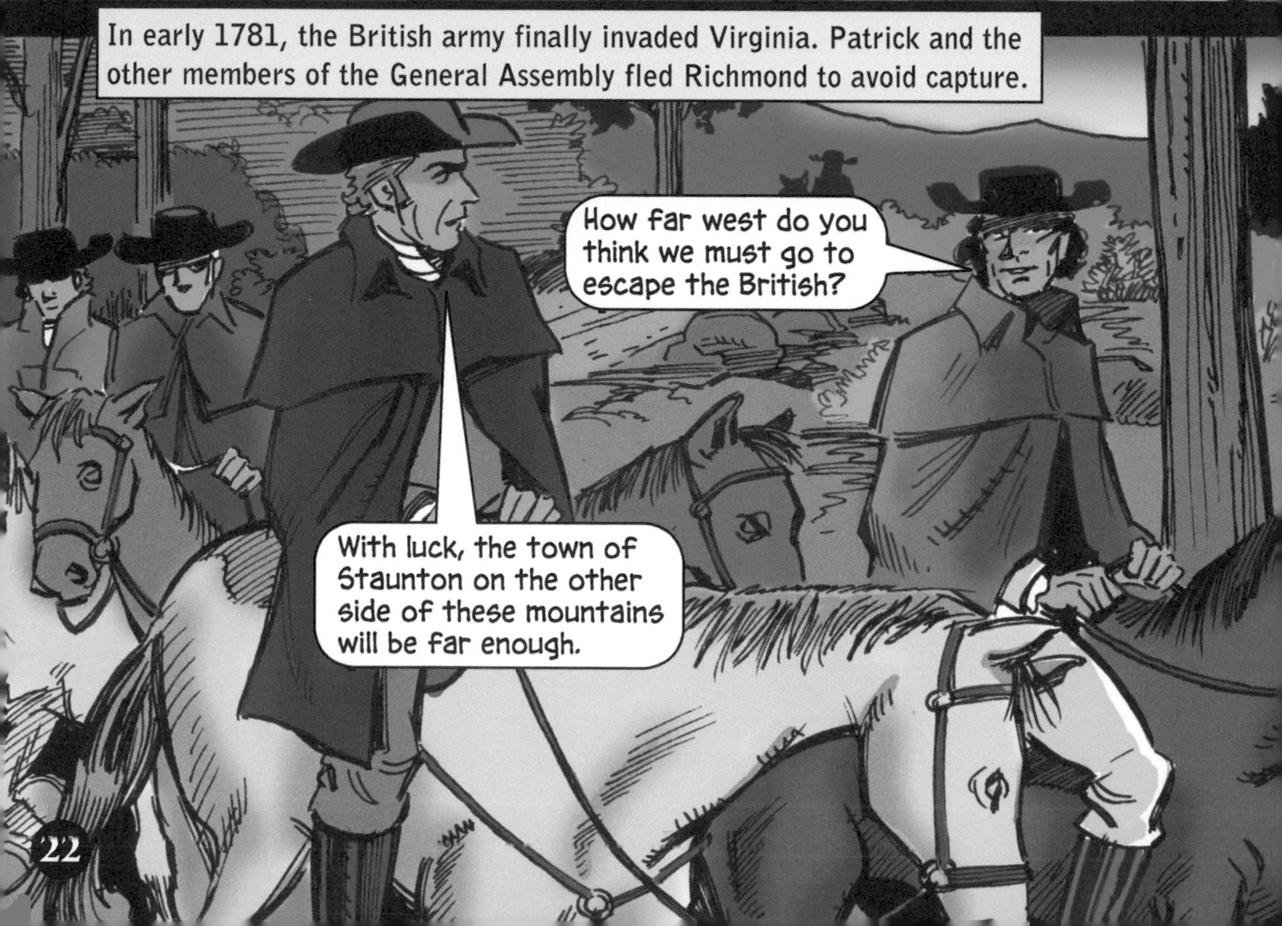
In early 1781, the British army finally invaded Virginia. Patrick and the other members of the General Assembly fled Richmond to avoid capture.
How far west do you think we must go to escape the British?
With luck, the town of Staunton on the other side of these mountains will be far enough.

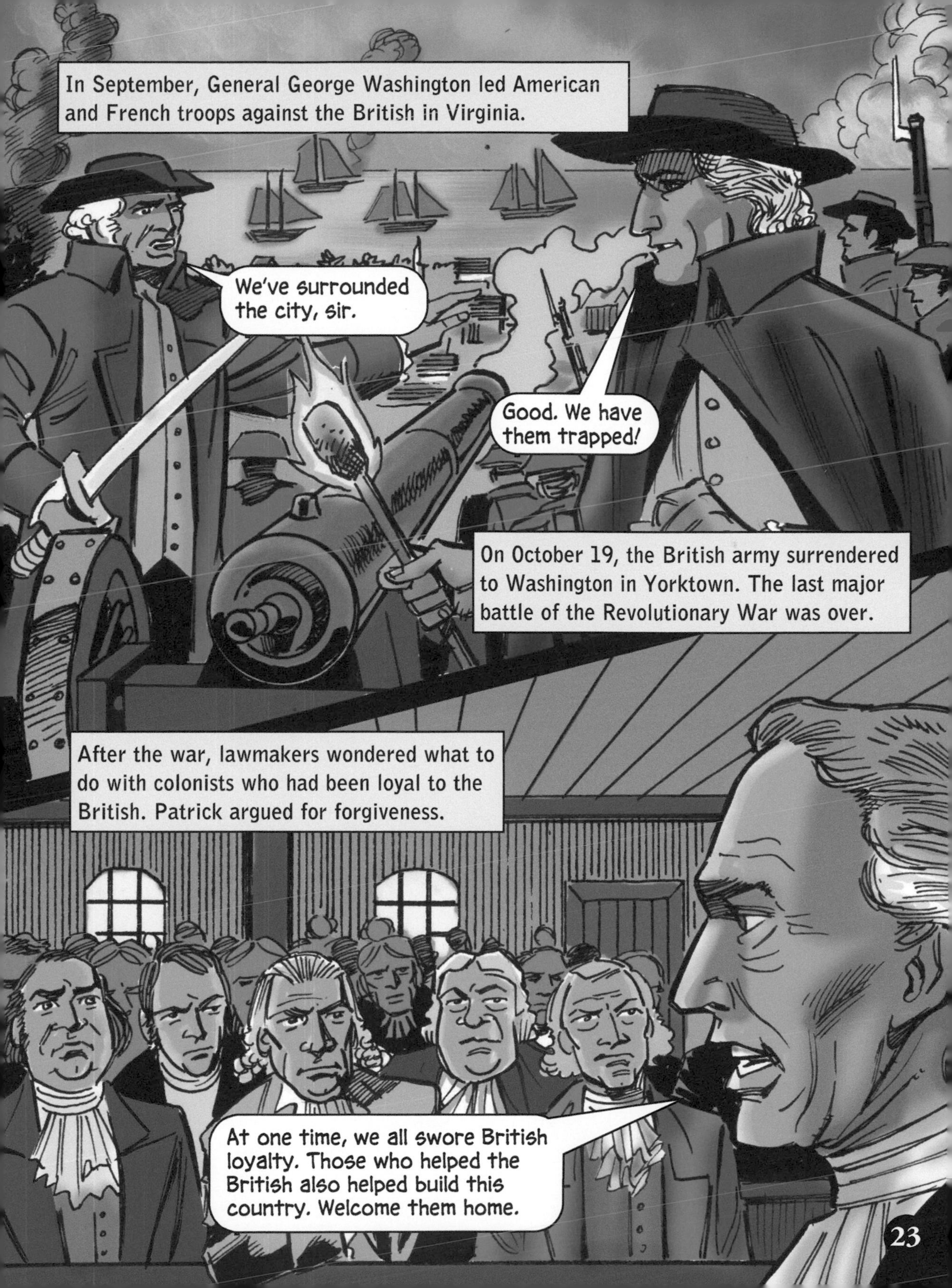
In September, General George Washington led American and French troops against the British in Virginia.
We've surrounded the city, sir.
Good. We have them trapped!
On October 19, the British army surrendered to Washington in Yorktown. The last major battle of the Revolutionary War was over.
After the war, lawmakers wondered what to do with colonists who had been loyal to the British. Patrick argued for forgiveness.
At one time, we all swore British loyalty. Those who helped the British also helped build this country. Welcome them home.

CHAPTER 4

FINAL YEARS OF SERVICE

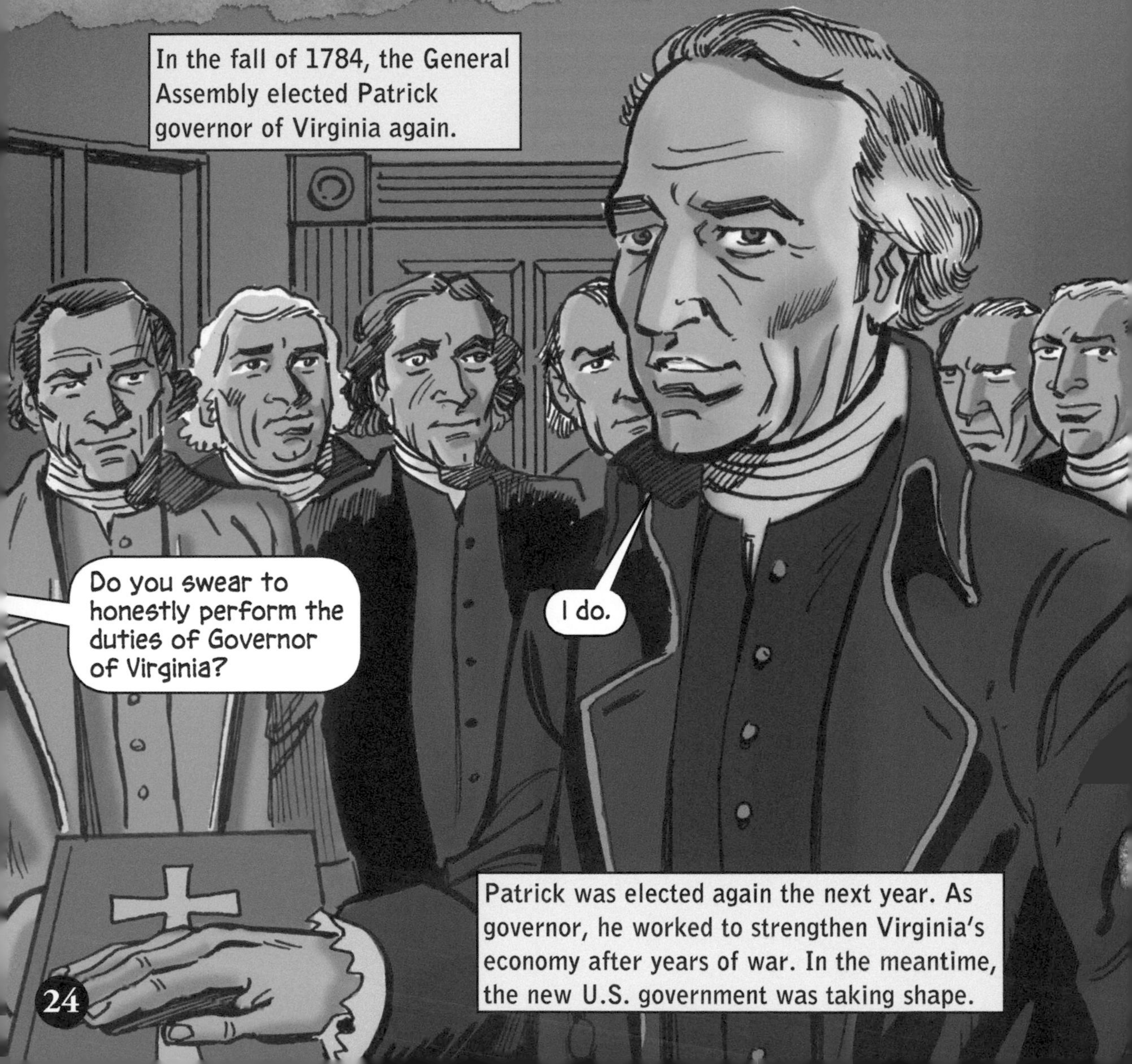
In the fall of 1784, the General Assembly elected Patrick governor of Virginia again.
Do you swear to honestly perform the duties of Governor of Virginia?
I do.
Patrick was elected again the next year. As governor, he worked to strengthen Virginia's economy after years of war. In the meantime, the new U.S. government was taking shape.

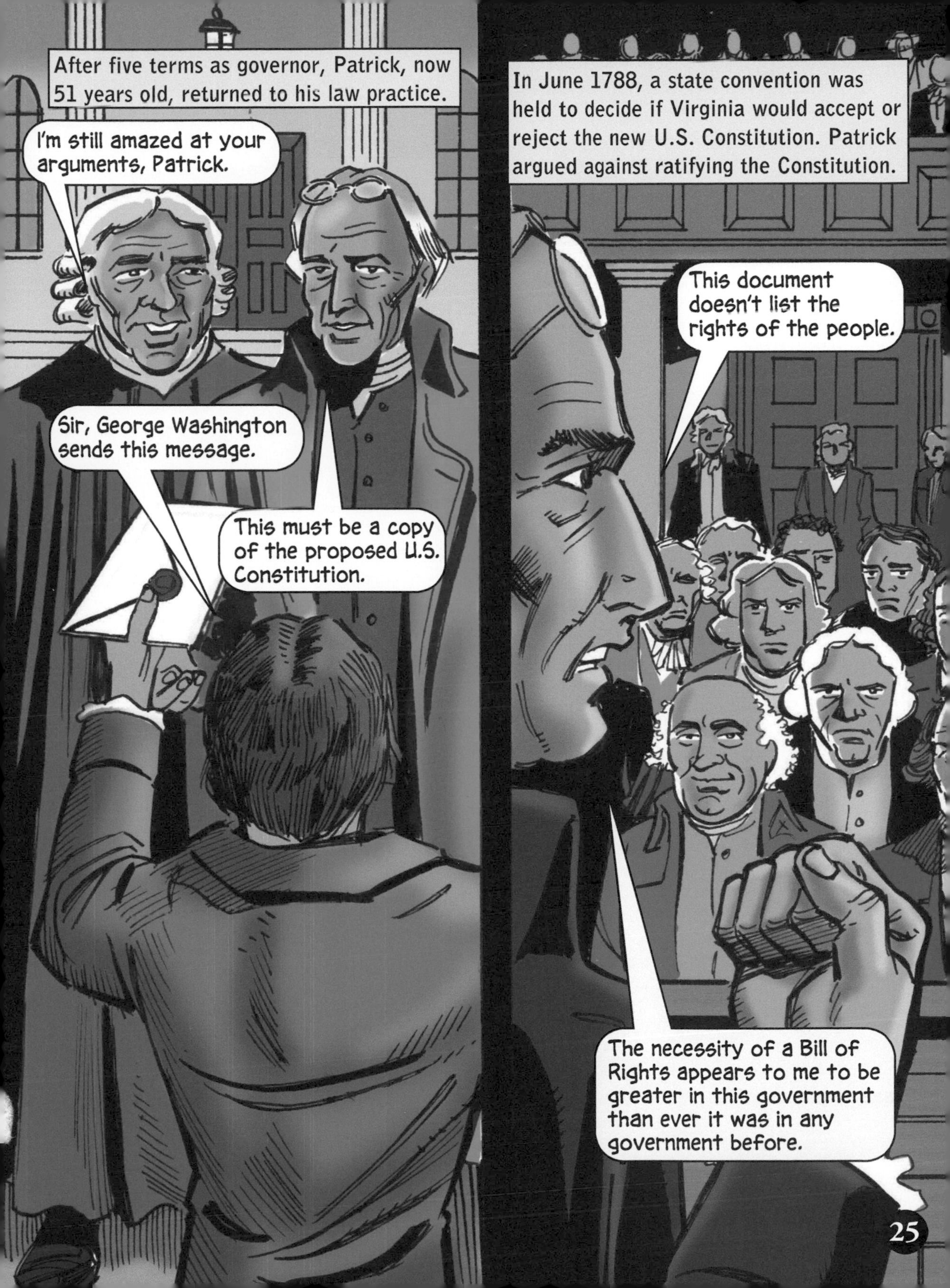
After five terms as governor, Patrick, now 51 years old, returned to his law practice.
I'm still amazed at your arguments, Patrick.
Sir, George Washington sends this message.
This must be a copy of the proposed U.S. Constitution.
In June 1788, a state convention was held to decide if Virginia would accept or reject the new U.S. Constitution. Patrick argued against ratifying the Constitution.
This document doesn't list the rights of the people.
The necessity of a Bill of Rights appears to me to be greater in this government than ever it was in any government before.

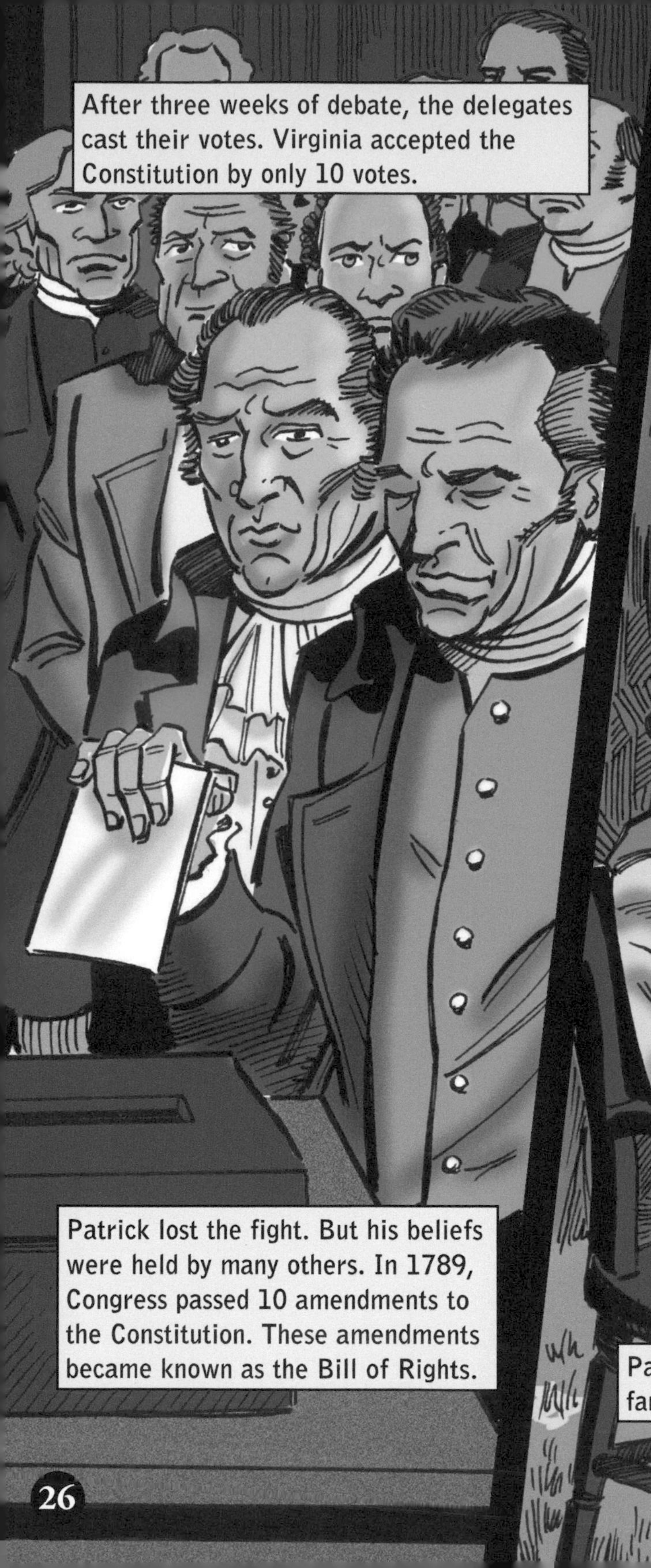
After three weeks of debate, the delegates cast their votes. Virginia accepted the Constitution by only 10 votes.
Patrick lost the fight. But his beliefs were held by many others. In 1789, Congress passed 10 amendments to the Constitution. These amendments became known as the Bill of Rights.

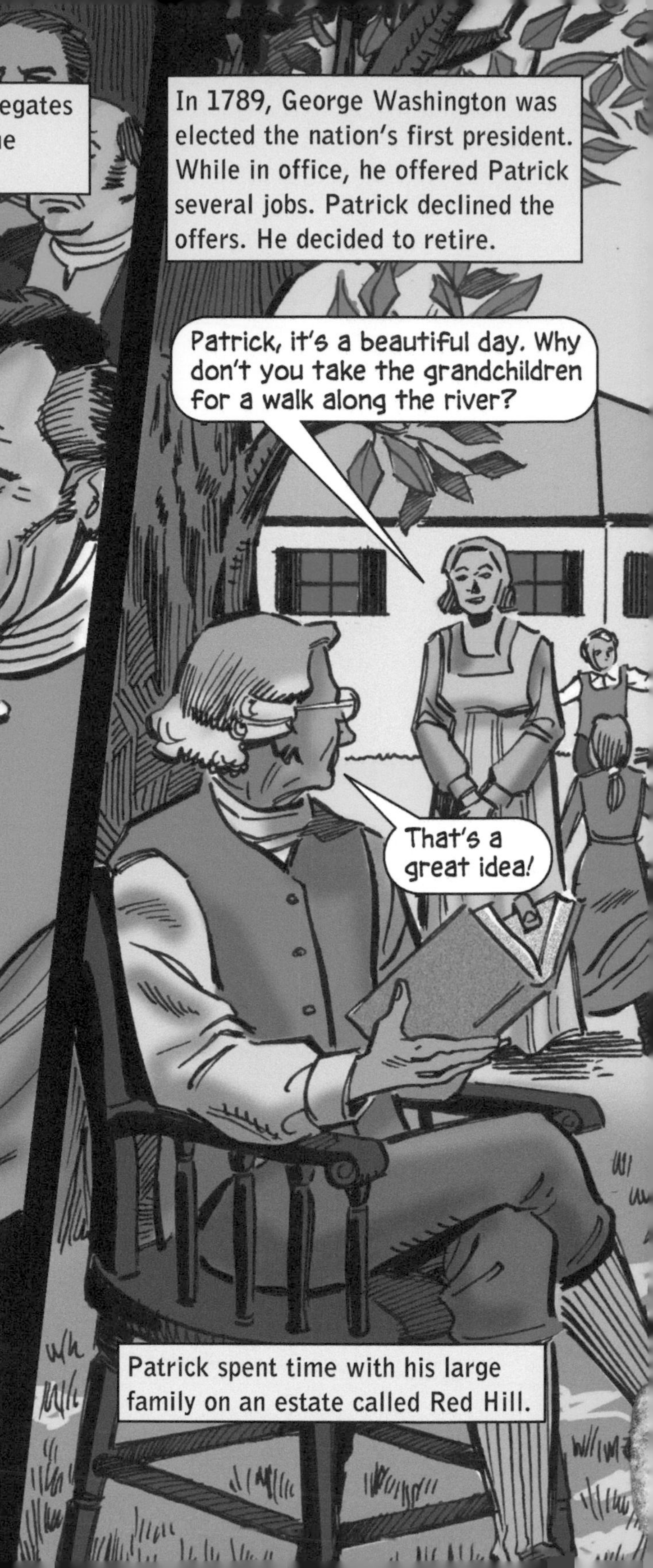
In 1789, George Washington was elected the nation's first president. While in office, he offered Patrick several jobs. Patrick declined the offers. He decided to retire.
Patrick, it's a beautiful day. Why don't you take the grandchildren for a walk along the river?
That's a great idea!
Patrick spent time with his large family on an estate called Red Hill.

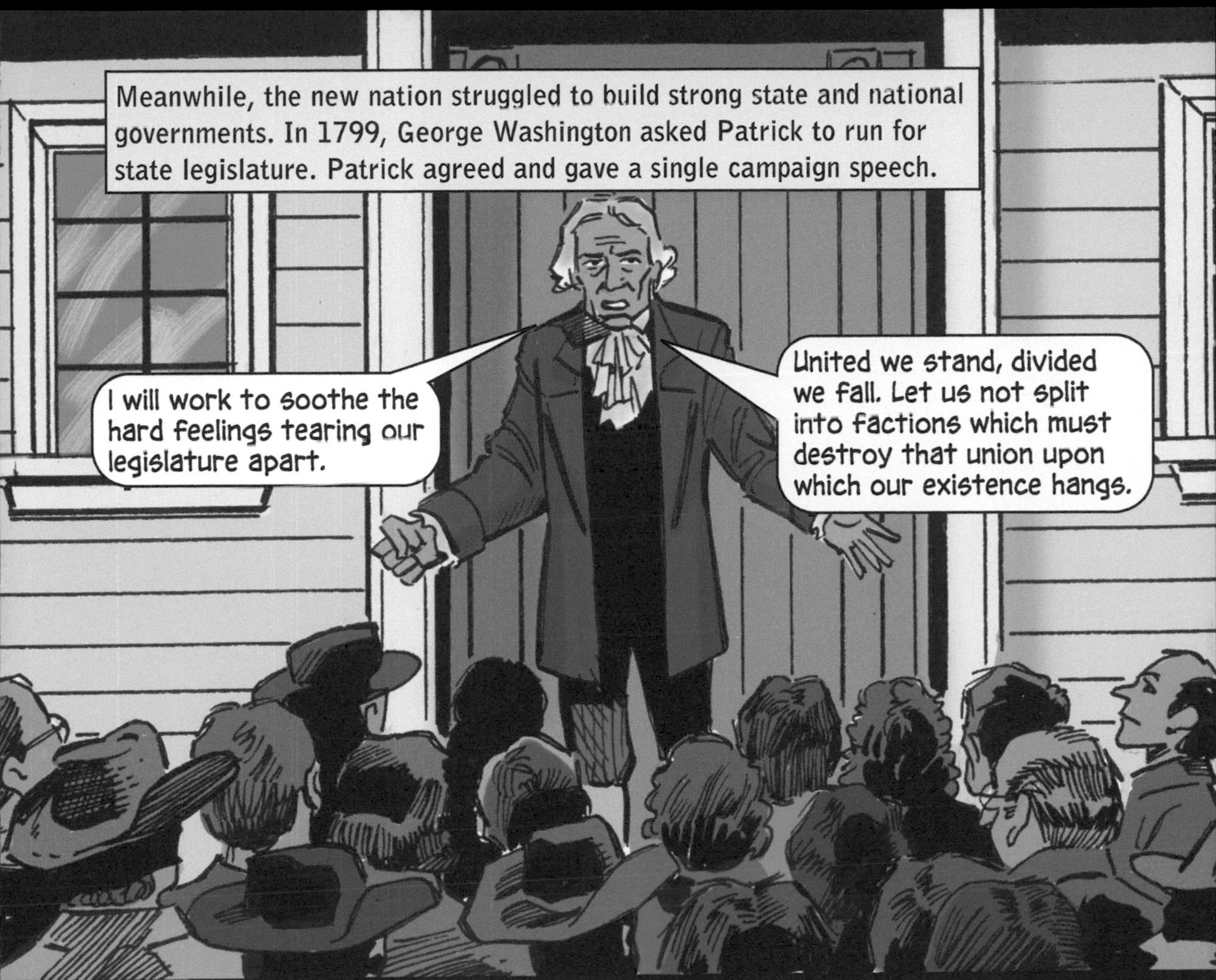
Meanwhile, the new nation struggled to build strong state and national governments. In 1799, George Washington asked Patrick to run for state legislature. Patrick agreed and gave a single campaign speech.
I will work to soothe the hard feelings tearing our legislature apart.
United we stand, divided we fall. Let us not split into factions which must destroy that union upon which our existence hangs.

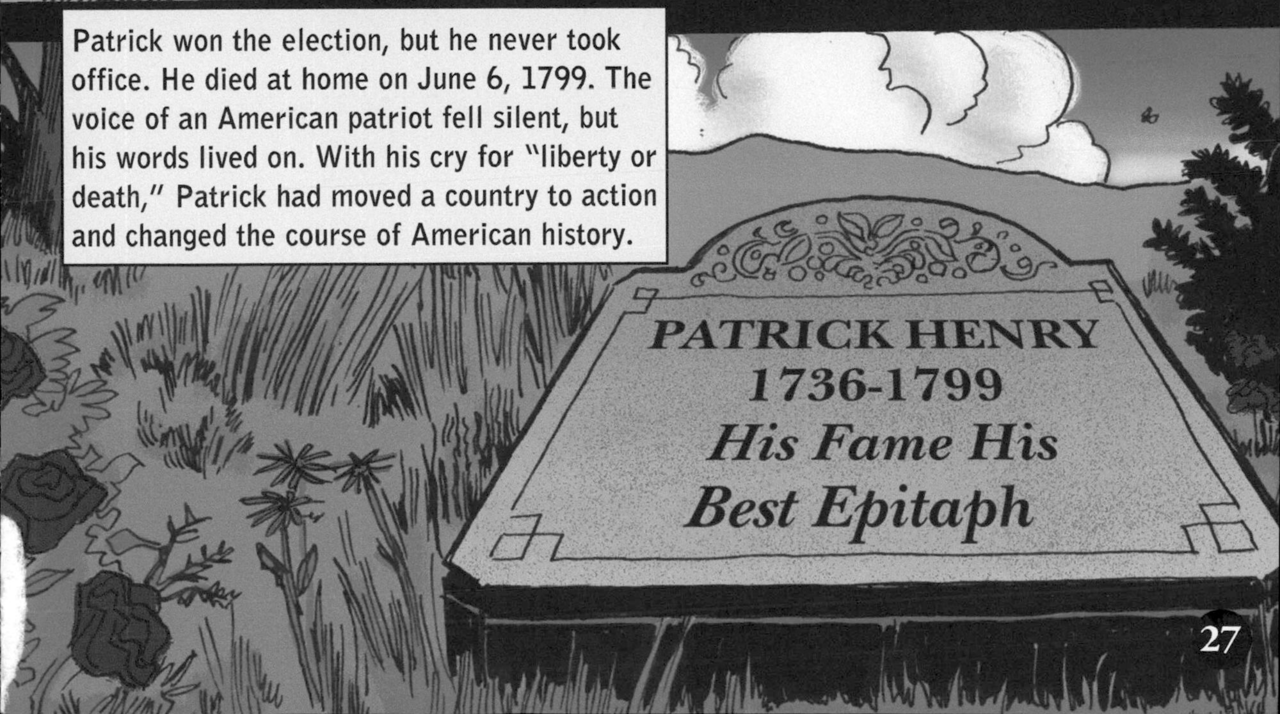
Patrick won the election, but he never took office. He died at home on June 6, 1799. The voice of an American patriot fell silent, but his words lived on. With his cry for "liberty or death," Patrick had moved a country to action and changed the course of American history.
PATRICK HENRY
1736-1799
His Fame His
Best Epitaph

MORE ABOUT PATRICK HENRY

◆ Patrick Henry was born May 29, 1736, in Hanover County, Virginia. He died June 6, 1799, at the age of 63.

◆ With Patrick's help, Kentucky became a county of Virginia in 1776. It became its own state in 1792.

◆ Patrick became a colonel of Virginia's First Regiment and commander of Virginia's regular forces in August 1775. His soldiers liked him, but some members of Virginia's government didn't think he had enough military experience. As a result, his regiment wasn't given many missions. After five months in the military, Patrick resigned.

◆ Patrick had only been in the House of Burgesses for nine days before he presented his Stamp Act Resolutions.

◆ Patrick had 17 children. He had six children with his first wife, Sarah, and 11 with his second wife, Dorothea.

◆ Patrick helped to start Hampden Sydney College in Virginia. He believed that it was the duty of the state to educate its citizens.

- Patrick fought hard for a Bill of Rights to be added to the U.S. Constitution. In 1789, 10 amendments, known as the Bill of Rights, were added to the Constitution. One of these amendments granted all citizens the rights of freedom of religion, speech, and the press.

- Patrick turned down several job offers after he retired to Red Hill. These jobs included Chief Justice of the Supreme Court, Secretary of State, and minister to Spain and to France.

- With Patrick's will, his family found a copy of his Stamp Act Resolutions. On the back was written "Reader! Whoever thou art, remember this . . . practice virtue thyself, and encourage it in others."

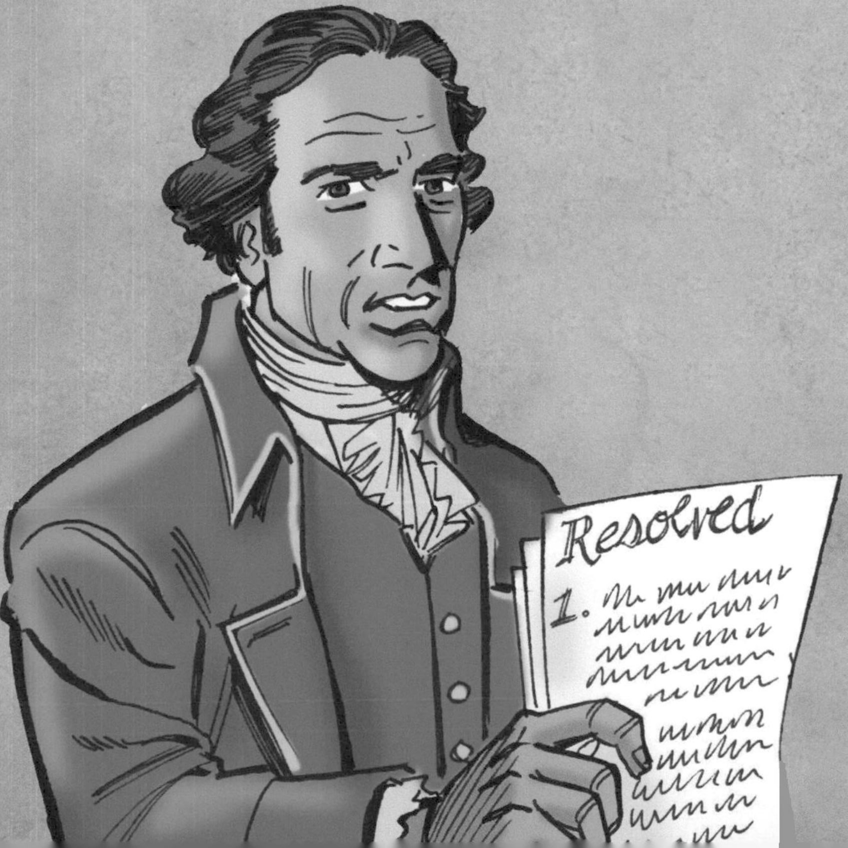
Resolved
1.

GLOSSARY

damages (DAM-ij-ees)—money given to people by a court of law to make up for an injury or a loss they have suffered

parliament (PAR-luh-muhnt)—the governing body that makes the laws in Britain

pound (POUND)—a unit of money used in England and several other countries; also a unit of weight equal to 16 ounces.

resolution (rez-uh-LOO-shuhn)—a formal statement of an opinion or decision

treason (TREE-zuhn)—betraying one's country, especially by helping the enemy or plotting to overthrow the government

tyrant (TYE-ruhnt)—someone who rules other people in a cruel or unjust way

INTERNET SITES

FactHound offers a safe, fun way to find Internet sites related to this book. All of the sites on FactHound have been researched by our staff.

Here's how:

1. Visit *www.facthound.com*
2. Type in this special code **073684970X** for age-appropriate sites. Or enter a search word related to this book for a more general search.
3. Click on the **Fetch It** button.

FactHound will fetch the best sites for you!

READ MORE

Kukla, Amy, and John Kukla. *Patrick Henry: Voice of the Revolution.* The Library of American Lives and Times. New York: PowerKids Press, 2002.

Marquette, Scott. *Revolutionary War.* America at War. Vero Beach, Fla.: Rourke, 2003.

McPherson, Stephanie Sammartino. *Liberty or Death: A Story about Patrick Henry.* A Creative Minds Biography. Minneapolis: Carolrhoda Books, 2003.

Williams, Jean Kinney. *The U.S. Constitution.* We the People. Minneapolis: Compass Point Books, 2004.

BIBLIOGRAPHY

Meade, Robert Douthat. *Patrick Henry: Patriot in the Making.* Philadelphia: J. B. Lippincott, 1957.

Meade, Robert Douthat. *Patrick Henry: Practical Revolutionary.* Philadelphia: J. B. Lippincott, 1969.

Tyler, Moses Coit. *Patrick Henry.* Ithaca, N.Y.: Great Seal Books, 1962.

Willison, George F. *Patrick Henry and His World.* Garden City, N.Y.: Doubleday, 1969.

INDEX